Hypnotism: A Complete System of Method, Application and Use

(1900)

Contents: The Science of Hypnotism; Instructions for Testing Subjects; Inducing Hypnotic Sleep; Fascination; Celebrated Table Method; Stage Purposes; The Lock Method; Post-Hypnotic Suggestion; Anaesthesia; Cataleptic or Rigid State; Lethargic or Independent State; clairvoyant or Second Sight; Self-Induced Hypnosis; To Hypnotize by Telegraph, Telephone of Mail; People Hypnotized Against their Will; Hindoo Sleep—How Induced; Symptons of Hypnotism; How to Make a Subject; Curing Disease by Hypnotism; Personal Magnetism; Insanity; Animals; Magnetic Healing; plus much more.

L.W. de Laurence

ISBN 1-56459-925-6

Kessinger Publishing's
Rare Mystical Reprints

THOUSANDS OF SCARCE BOOKS ON THESE AND OTHER SUBJECTS:

Freemasonry * Akashic * Alchemy * Alternative Health * Ancient Civilizations * Anthroposophy * Astrology * Astronomy * Aura * Bible Study * Cabalah * Cartomancy * Chakras * Clairvoyance * Comparative Religions * Divination * Druids * Eastern Thought * Egyptology * Esoterism * Essenes * Etheric * ESP * Gnosticism * Great White Brotherhood * Hermetics * Kabalah * Karma * Knights Templar * Kundalini * Magic * Meditation * Mediumship * Mesmerism * Metaphysics * Mithraism * Mystery Schools * Mysticism * Mythology * Numerology * Occultism * Palmistry * Pantheism * Parapsychology * Philosophy * Prosperity * Psychokinesis * Psychology * Pyramids * Qabalah * Reincarnation * Rosicrucian * Sacred Geometry * Secret Rituals * Secret Societies * Spiritism * Symbolism * Tarot * Telepathy * Theosophy * Transcendentalism * Upanishads * Vedanta * Wisdom * Yoga * *Plus Much More!*

DOWNLOAD A FREE CATALOG AT:
www.kessinger.net

OR EMAIL US AT:
books@kessinger.net

PREFACE.

In bringing before the public this book on Hypnotism, Mesmerism, and Suggestive Therapeutics, or the treatment of disease by Hypnotism and Suggestion, I feel that no apology is necessary for introducing so important a subject.

No method of treatment has during the last few years attracted so much interest among men of science and members of the medical profession, as has the science of Hypnotism and Suggestion.

The dangers of Hypnotism and Mesmerism have been proven chimerical; and are merely imaginary, for in proper hands no undesirable medical results can occur through its practice, and there is, I believe, hardly one authenticated case of its being used for a criminal purpose in the countries where it is extensively used, especially by the medical profession. More than this can hardly be said of any system of medical treatment. The treatment of disease by Hypnotism and Suggestion has been very successful where it has been practiced by qualified physicians and intelligent operators whose knowledge and experience has taught them the use of Hypnotism and Mesmerism in its practical application, and many noted physicians unhesitatingly advocate its use as a powerful auxiliary in combating many forms of nervous and other diseases, not readily reached by other means.

Hypnotism and Mesmerism, so called, consists of a true knowledge of the science of the human mind, or soul.

The mistake the medical fraternity have and are making is that they have made an exhaustive and scientific study of the physical or material part of the human organism, but not of the immaterial part; they analyze and dissect the physical body, but seem to have no realization or knowledge of the non-physical part, or soul of man.

The mind controls the physical body, the body being merely a register or an indicator of mental conditions, or the actual condition of the mind; therefore it is essential that every physician should have a thorough knowledge of pyschology (Hypnotism and Mesmerism) as well as physiology, which is a scientific knowledge of the mind and its relation to the human body.

Bodily disease is always mental in origin, mental in action, mental in character, and mental in cure, and but for the action of the life or vital forces on the diseased organs and functions of the body no disease would ever be cured. The physician gives medicine to, as he says, assist nature, which consists of the life and vital forces, or mind, of which he has no true knowledge.

Hypnotism and Suggestion is the fundamental principle of curing and healing every disease. No matter what other means may be employed, when nature or the life forces within the body fails to react on the diseased functions and organs, all the medicine and physicians in the universe cannot effect a cure, or prevent a death.

Observing people do not always have time to wander through a perplexing multitude of books in a fruitless attempt to gain a little knowledge buried therein. The instructions and methods given here are the latest and most complete known for inducing the Mesmeric and Hypnotic sleep. Nothing problematical is given; but facts gained from personal experience by the author in the successful practice of Hypnotism, Mesmerism, Suggestive Therapeutics, and Magnetic Healing, for many years.

Many conceited and narrow-minded individuals look upon Hypnotism as a fraud.

"Seest thou a man wise in his own conceit,
There is more hope of a fool than of him."
(Prov. 26:12.)

The fact that complete anaethsia can be produced in any part of the body, provides the experimenter with a ready means of demonstrating that there is no simulation on the part of the subject.

There are two things for this class of people to learn yet: First, that a statement that they do not believe in Hypnotism or Magnetism brands them as being ignorant and destitute of a knowledge of Psychology,

And that to ridicule what you do not understand is what really wise men never do.

The author does not wish to be understood as attacking the teaching of materia medica, or antagonizing the medical profession, but as suggesting a way by which they may be rendered more effectual and potent by a study and better understanding of Psycho-Therapeutics.

This book will be of great value and interest to the physician, clergyman, lawyer, teacher, merchant, and the private citizen of either sex, and will, I trust, be a useful hand-book for practitioners and those who have not the time to devote to more elaborate and systematic works.

The Author.

"Hypnotism embodies and unfolds the law and secret power, by which and through which all personal influence is and ever shall be exerted."

DE LAURENCE.

"All that we are or ever will be is the result of what has been thought."

DE LAURENCE.

CONTENTS.

	PAGE
PREFACE	7
THE SCIENCE OF HYPNOTISM	17
INSTRUCTIONS FOR TESTING SUBJECTS	23
INDUCING HYPNOTIC SLEEP	27
FASCINATION	33
CELEBRATED TABLE METHOD	35
FOR STAGE PURPOSES	37
THE LOCK METHOD	41
THE FAMOUS NANCY METHOD	43
POST-HYPNOTIC SUGGESTIONS	45
ANAESTHESIA—HOW PRODUCED	49
CATALEPTIC OR RIGID STATE	53
LETHARGIC OR INDEPENDENT STATE	57
CLAIRVOYANT OR SECOND SIGHT	59
HYPNOSIS SELF-INDUCED	65
TO HYPNOTIZE BY TELEGRAPH, TELEPHONE OR MAIL	73
PEOPLE HYPNOTIZED AGAINST THEIR WILL	77
INSTANTLY HYPNOTISED	81
HINDOO SLEEP—HOW INDUCED	83
SYMPTOMS OF HYPNOSIS	89
DIFFERENT STAGES OF HYPNOSIS	91

CONTENTS.

	PAGE
How to Make a Subject	93
Curing Disease by Hypnotism	95
Personal Magnetism	97
Hypnotism and Crime	101
Hypnotism and Insanity	107
Hypnotizing Animals	111
Hypnotizing by a Rotating Mirror	115
Mind and Body, or The Science of Being	117
Telepathy, Mind Reading and Spiritualism	125
Magnetic Healing	143
The Phenomena of Hypnosis	153
The Psychology of Hypnosis	161
Treatment by Hypnotism and Suggestion	169

HYPNOTISM.

CHAPTER I.

THE SCIENCE OF HYPNOTISM.

INTRODUCTION.

Hypnotism and Mesmerism, its History.—Brief Sketch of the Life of Friedrich Anton Mesmer—Discovery of Animal Magnetism.—Mesmer's Passes.—Hypnotism a Psychological not a Physiological Condition—Definition of Hypnotism, Mesmerism, and Animal, or Personal, Magnetism.—Terms Used.

The science of Hypnotism and Mesmerism has been evolved from such a labyrinth of idle superstition and wild speculation that even those keenly interested in the development of human knowledge have held aloof from a subject which apparently presents so entangled a maze of insoluble complications.

In the long course of its history it has been the frequent prey of the unscientific investigator, and, indeed almost everybody ignorant of its true principle, has a theory or idea as to how the phenomena is produced. The history of Hypnotism begins almost like a fable. Methods were in use amongst the Egyptians, the Greeks, and the Romans, which present a striking similarity to the means adopted by modern Hypnotists.

In the British museum there is a bas-relief taken from a tomb in Thebes. The "Subject," as he would be termed in modern phraseology, is sitting down, and a short distance from him a man is standing with hand uplifted and evidently about to make a pass over the subject. The Goddess Isis, on the zodiac of her temple, at Denderah, is represented as making the same "Passes" the earliest Greek physicians were in the habit of using, processes having a strong resemblance to those used by every Hypnotist.

The first traces of any system appeared about the end of the middle ages, and then it was attempted to demonstrate that the human will was capable of producing the phenomena.

It then remained for Mesmer to shed new light upon the question, and in 1775 he discovered that the phenomena could be produced in various ways, and then it was called Mesmerism, but was afterwards changed to Hypnotism, in 1841, by Dr. Braid of England, who produced

HYPNOTIC SLEEP INDUCED INSTANTLY.

the phenomena by a different method, and called the condition produced Hypnosis (a Greek word meaning sleep) and the art of producing it Hypnotism.

To those, however, who would have a clear knowledge of what Hypnotism is and what it is not, a study of its history is not essential. And it is quite an easy matter to teach any one how to hypnotize. Any person of ordinary intelligence can be taught to become a successful operator by simply following the methods herein described, which, if strictly obeyed, will enable any one to succeed.

In order to make plain to the student certain phrases and terms which I shall use in this work, it will be necessary to call attention to a brief sketch of the history of Hypnotism and Mesmerism.

Mesmerism takes its name from Friedrich Anton Mesmer, who was born in a village called Stein, on the banks of the Rhine, in May, 1734, and was educated and attained his degree of Dr. at Vienna, where he studied under Professor Van Switen and Professor Haen.

In 1775 he startled the world by reports of his discovery of what is now known as Personal or Animal Magnetism. He operated by a system of passes demonstrating the existence of personal magnetism, and that magnetism could be directed by the will of the operator to the subject, and that this influence was capable when properly and intelligently directed of producing the phenomena known now as Mesmerism, or the mesmeric sleep.

Later, in 1841, Dr. Braid of England, the famous Manchester physician, produced the phenomena by an entirely different method. His method of operating consisted of fixation of gaze, and he and many others supposed the cause and condition was a purely physiological one.

This view, as is known by all enlightened and learned men in Psychology, is a mistaken one. As all Hypnotic, Mesmeric and abnormal states are caused and brought about by actual psychical condition, whether self-induced or otherwise. The phenomena known as Hypnosis is not a physiological condition, and all views to this effect are erroneous.

Very few are aware of the difference between Hypnotism and Mesmerism, and many confound the two as meaning the same thing. It is essential for the student to know that all conditions induced by the subject fixing his gaze on an object, either held in the hand of the operator or not is an hypnotic state, and that all conditions induced by passes or any other personal application or direction of the will by the operator is a mesmeric state. Practically speaking, the condition or state induced and the phenomena produced by either means is the same, both being a purely psychical condition, and consists of an entire suspension of the physical sense organs, whether brought about by mesmeric passes, concentration of gaze, fascination, or any other means, and while in this condition the subject is under the control of the operator and susceptible to Suggestion.

The study of Hypnotism from a psychological point is absolutely essential to success, and the importance of a careful observation of the phenomena of Hypnotism and its relation to the psychic mind can hardly be exaggerated. And for the student of Hypnotism or Psychology there is a wide field of work where the opportunities for definite experimental work are many. This view could have been more employed than it has been up to the present time, as too many writers on Psychology, appear to think that a casual acquaintance with the subject is all that is necessary as a basis of opinion. Hypnotism or its results are based upon natural law. It is, "The science of the age," and the most interesting of all the sciences. And any one who studies the human mind from a psychological point of view and learns its influence over the human body, has a wonderful advantage.

Strictly speaking, the difference between Hypnotism and Mesmerism, or the Mesmeric or Hypnotic sleep, is that sleep induced by passes as used by Mesmer is termed the Mesmeric or Magnetic sleep, and sleep induced by objective gaze, where the subject concentrates his mind and sight upon some certain object until Hypnosis is induced is termed the Hypnotic sleep. To avoid confusion, however, I will dispense with these several different terms for the phenomena whether Hypnotic, Mesmeric or Magnetic, is commonly known as Hypnotism. I will use this term especially in the body part of the instructions contained in this book as specifying these different phenomena. And the different conditions when induced as an Hypnosis or Hypnotic state.

CHAPTER II.

INSTRUCTIONS FOR TESTING SUBJECTS.

Who is Susceptible to Hypnosis.—Who Make Good Subjects.—Concentration Necessary—Favorite Methods. Hand and Eye Test.—Breaking the Influence.—Drawing Test—Difficult Subjects.—Vain Struggle.

As some persons are more quickly influenced than others, being more susceptible to hypnotic influence, you can by the following methods easily ascertain what ones will make good subjects and whether you will be able to impress them or not.

First have the subject you are going to test stand up in the center of the room, place both arms down by his side with his heels touching, and ask him to let, as far as possible, his muscles relax and to stand perfectly still.

Now take a position in front of the subject and tell him you are going to draw him forward, but not to be afraid of falling as you will stop him before he reaches the floor. Now concentrate your gaze intently and directly on the pupil of his left eye, and hold the thought and intention firmly in your mind that you are going to draw him over toward you, and while looking at him do not let any other thought or idea enter your mind, or nothing divert your attention from the task you have before you. Stand quite close to the subject, raise both of your open hands to the level of his eyes opposite either side of his head, fingers pointing backward, concentrate your eyes on his, as directed above, and draw your hands steadily and firmly forward all the while intently willing him forward.

Repeat this method if you do not succeed the first time in influencing him, being sure to get the proper concentration.

If the subject is susceptible to Hypnosis he will feel an influence drawing him forward off from his balance that he cannot resist. You can now take the same position at his back and operate on his head at the base of the brain in the same manner that you did in front of him, drawing him backward off from his balance and catching him with your hands, at the same time saying, "All right; all right."

Another favorite method for testing a subject is to have the person you are going to operate on sit down in a chair and clasp his hands tightly together by crossing the fingers, with arms extended straight out from the shoulder.

Take a position in front of him and clasp his

hands between the thumb and second finger of your left hand, and with your right hand make passes down over his arms, touching them lightly from the shoulders to the hands. Keeping your gaze riveted on his left eye and give the following suggestions in a firm voice and decided manner, say to him your hands are getting tighter together all the time. Your hands are getting tighter, tighter, all the time. Now when you try to get your hands apart you cannot do it; you will find the more you try the tighter your hands will stick. Now step back. releasing his hands, and he will find it a physical impossibility to get his hands apart. And when he is satisfied you have got his hands locked tightly together, release him from the influence by clapping your hands together or snapping your fingers and at the same time saying in a loud voice, "All right. Now you can take your hands apart; your hands are all right now."

The next is the eye test, and is a good one when properly made.

Seat the subject as before, with both feet flat upon the floor, tell him you are going to fix his eyes so he cannot get them open no matter how hard he tries. Now have him close his eyes and place his right hand palm downward on his right knee, grasp his open left hand in your left and with the fingers of your right hand make light passes or strokes over his eyes and forehead and give suggestions as follows:

"Now when you try to open your eyes you will find the lids are stuck so tightly together you cannot get them apart, and the more you try to get them apart the tighter they will stick, no matter how hard you try you cannot open your eyes." Now let him try but at the same time keep his left hand in yours and let him struggle in the vain effort to open his eyes. Tell him to stand up and see if he can open them, and when you wish to release him do so by clapping your hands or snapping your fingers and saying, "All right now."

If a subject is influenced by any of the above tests, he can safely be regarded as a good subject for demonstrations in Hypnotism, but if he has not been in the least influenced or affected by any of the tests you may regard him as a difficult subject, and one that will take time and patience to influence, and cannot be used right away.

CHAPTER III.

FOR INDUCING HYPNOTIC SLEEP.

METHOD ONE.

Disturbing Influence.—Undue Nervousness.—Precautions Necessary.—Precautions Dispensable—Constant Suggestions.—Suggested Catalepsy.—Reversing Passes.—Somnambulism.—Changed Personality.—Variety of Delusions.

"Man has the faculty of exercising over his fellow beings a salutary influence by concentrating his mind and will upon what he desires them to do."—DeLaurence.

To induce Hypnotic sleep proceed as follows: Have the subject sit in a comfortable chair with his back to the light, assuming an easy natural position for sleep, placing his feet upon the floor, and the open palms of his hands upon each knee; never have the hands or legs crossed when inducing Hypnosis. Now take a position on his right side, and state to him that you are going to put him into a sound comfortable sleep. Tell him to let every muscle in his body become perfectly relaxed, and just think to himself that he is getting so sleepy that he cannot keep his eyes open. Then, secure the subject's attention; and hold it. Let him see by your behavior and easy, confident manner that you are competent and master of the situation; assert that you can hypnotize him, and you will be successful. Do not let the thought of failure enter your mind for one moment, and do not be afraid to make positive assertions, but state, "You can, and will, Hypnotize him."

Now concentrate your gaze and mind on the pupil of his left eye and tell him not to let his eyes waver or try to avoid your eyes, but to look at you all the time—until his eyes get so sleepy he cannot keep them open.

Now all the while constantly willing him to sleep give the following suggestions by saying, "You will begin to feel a sleepy, drowsy sensation coming all over your body; you will feel a sleepy influence coming all over your head and eyes; you are getting sleepy, sleepy, sleepy, so sleepy and drowsy you will not be able to keep your eyes open; your eyelids are getting so heavy you cannot keep them up. You are going sound asleep, sleep, sleep, so sleepy and drowsy; you're getting so sleepy and drowsy you cannot keep your eyes open any longer." Repeat the above suggestions over and over until you notice the subject's eyes getting so sleepy and drowsy that he cannot keep them open. Then say, "Sound asleep." "Dead asleep." "Down deep asleep." "Go deep." "Down deep." And when his eyes are closed make light passes over the forehead and eyes, touching them very lightly, but keep on giving the suggestions of deep sleep. Say to him, "Every breath you draw puts you down deeper asleep, every breath you draw is a sleepy and drowsy one; every part of your body is sound asleep, dead asleep, dead asleep."

If the subject's eyes do not close entirely, although he looks and feels sleepy, press down the eye lids with the tips of your fingers and he will be sound asleep.

Have everybody present keep perfectly quiet. The surroundings must be free from any disturbing influences and noises like the quiet opening or shutting of a door, or the whispering of persons inside the room. All these serve to distract the attention of the subject at a critical time. The subject should be asked to keep his mind a blank as far as possible, and not trouble his mind over anything. Every thing should be done to have the subject calm and free from undue nervousness.

It must not be assumed that these detailed observances are in all cases necessary, for it greatly depends upon the susceptibility of the subject, but if you expect to gain an average of anything over 80 per cent it will only be by attention to these details. The first Hypnosis is always the most difficult to induce, and after the subject has been hypnotized a few times you can generally dispense with a great many of these precautions.

You now have the subject sound asleep, and it will be well for you, as a beginner, especially if you have a new subject, constantly to make suggestions, as follows: You say, "Now you are fast asleep; nothing will disturb you or wake you. You cannot wake up until I count three and wake you up. You can open your eyes, but you will stay asleep. Nothing will wake you."

You can now induce what is termed

SUGGESTED CATALEPSY.

In the following manner: Place the arm straight out from the body; make passes from the shoulder to fingers, and say: "Now, your arm is stiff and rigid; you have no feeling in any part of your arm, and it will remain in the position I have placed it; you cannot take it down, no matter how hard you try."

The arm will remain in this position, and if you tell him that no one can take it down or bend it you will find it true that no one can. Always begin operation in this way, placing both arms in the upright position. When you are ready to take them down, make strokes from hand to shoulder, reversing them, and say: "Now you can take them down. And you will do everything I tell you; you will have to do so. No one can wake you except myself."

You can now proceed to induce somnambulism or trance condition, thereby changing the personality of the subject. Tell him that he will open his eyes without waking up, and when he opens his eyes he will behold the most beautiful flowers he ever saw, that there is a bed of them right in front of him, and tell him to pick some of them for you. And if he hesitates, insist. Tell him to get some for you, and have him give some one present an imaginary bouquet, or tell him a lot of bees are stinging him, and his frantic efforts to drive them off will be amusing; or give him a stick, for a pole, and have him catch some fish from an imaginary stream; or tell him he is a great politician, and have him make a speech to an imaginary audience; give him a lemon and tell him it is an orange or an apple and he will eat it with pleasure; give him suggestions that he is a little boy, and he will act out the part. Any delusion can be induced, and the variety depends on the imagination and descriptive powers of the operator.

You can make him forget his name, fix him so he cannot utter a word or open his mouth or make his limbs stiff so he cannot walk, and he will find it impossible to take a step or remove his feet from the floor until you tell him he can do so, or be released by the proper suggestion.

CHAPTER IV.

FASCINATION.

METHOD TWO.

Magnetic Personality Used.—Vacant Stars.—Involuntary Hypnosis.

This method, introducing as it does a large amount of the personal element or personal magnetism of the operator, is a favorite one with those who prefer to use the mesmeric passes and methods.

Seat the subject in a comfortable position on one side of the room, the operator taking a position about twelve or fifteen feet away. Have the subject gaze steadily into the operator's eyes, who must all the while keep his gaze firmly fixed on those of the subject until the eyes of the subject take on a vacant and trancelike stare. When this takes place you have him under perfect control and can induce sleep by sharp and decided suggestions to that effect, and proceed to induce somnambulism or trance condition as in Method One. This method is somewhat risky, since, if the subject be difficult or refractory, the operator himself may involuntarily become hypnotized.

As I have knowledge of a number of instances where in using this method operators have found themselves developing decided symptoms of Hypnosis, but this can be avoided by determination on the operator's part.

CHAPTER V.

CELEBRATED TABLE METHOD.

METHOD THREE.

Frantic Efforts.—Perfect Concentration.—Roars of Laughter.

The Table Method, as this one is sometimes called, is very desirable, as it can be used at private parties and social gatherings, especially when operating upon young ladies, or giving demonstrations in Hypnotism.

Have the subject sit in a chair on the opposite side of a table with hands clasped and fingers locked, arms resting straight out upon the table, the operator also sitting in a chair on the opposite side of the table gazing intently and steadily into the eyes of the subject for about two minutes or more, then in a low decided tone tell the subject that when he tries to raise his arms from the table he cannot do it, and when you have made him powerless to lift his arms tell him he cannot get up from the chair, that he is stuck fast and the harder he tries the tighter he will stick, and his frantic efforts to do so will provoke a roar of laughter. The suggestions must be made decidedly and the concentration profess good results.

CHAPTER VI.

FOR STAGE PURPOSES.

METHOD FOUR.

Hypnotic Show.—Individual Application.—Fast and Fierce—Demonstrations Positive.—Boisterousness.

The following method will be found the proper one for giving a Hypnotic show. After getting eight or ten persons to come upon the stage to be hypnotized seat them in a half circle, feet flat upon the floor, with palms of their hands resting on either knee, tell them all to close their eyes and sit perfectly quiet and think of nothing but sleep.

Then in a loud deep voice suggest, "Sleep, sleep, you are going down deep asleep, down deep, go deep, deep, down deep." Passing from one end of the circle to the other lightly touching the eyes of each individual, tell them to take long deep breaths and they "will go deep asleep, dead asleep."

Then in a loud determined voice tell them when they try to open their eyes or wake up they cannot do it. If some open their eyes, tell them to again close their eyes and operate on them individually, giving them a strong application, and if you cannot fasten their eyes in this manner, ask them politely to leave the stage, as you have not the time to devote to them and can only use those who can be readily influenced. Then proceed and give a show, putting on the cataleptic state, hat pin and needle tests, cake walk, boxing match, etc.

A Hypnotic show to be a success must not be allowed to drag, but must be fast and fierce, with positive demonstrations, warm enough to melt scepticism, and drive away a frost. Get the people with you by being firm and gentlemanly but not boisterous.

Make a speech something like the following:

"Ladies and gentlemen, I desire to state, that Hypnotism is and can be used in many ways, and it is especially good where surgical operations are to be performed. Hypnotism is also useful in the treatment of nervous and functional disorders, such as rheumatism, neuralgia, tobacco and morphine habits.

"I wish also to state that I do not want anybody to come upon the stage to show that they cannot be hypnotized, as it is no honor. The same may be said of an idiot. Unsusceptibility to hypnotic influence is not a sign of intelligence, however much your ignorance of the matter may prompt you to think so, and unless you mean to conduct yourself in a gentlemanly, courteous manner, and not affect Hypnotism when you are not hypnotized, I do not want you to come upon the stage, as I have no use for the pretender or professional fakir."

CHAPTER VII.

THE LOCK METHOD.

METHOD FIVE.

Mysterious.—Never Before Given Before the Public.—Bolted Doors.—Painful Positions.—Psychic Forces.—Mind Upon Matter.

The most marvelous and mysterious of all psychic and spiritualistic phenomena is the wonderful Lock Method, known to but a very few operators, and I can truthfully state that it has never before been given to the public. The person who possesses this knowledge can while outside of a room or locked in a room in another part of the house or building, or outside of the house entirely, with all doors bolted and locked, hypnotize a number of persons inside of the room or building in the following manner:

Have two or three subjects sit beside each other upon chairs, have them clasp their hands and then say, "All ready now, everybody." Then the operator should leave the room, having some person lock the door. He can go to another room or out of the building, if desired, taking a position in a quiet place and mentally suggesting to himself that the subjects cannot get their hands apart. If necessary the operator can be locked in another room, and in about five or seven minutes he can return and it will be found that the subjects' hands are tightly fastened together. Another way is to stand the subjects in the middle of the room with arms outstretched, the operator proceeding as before, but should not remain away this time over three or five minutes as this is a very painful and tiring position for the arms to be in any length of time. The operator can by this method demonstrate that for psychic forces or personal magnetism there exists no space, and that a person can be influenced at a distance as well as in the same room providing the proper conditions are brought about. There being an immediate action of psychic forces upon psychic forces, and not, as a common view takes for granted of mind upon matter.

CHAPTER VIII.

THE FAMOUS NANCY METHOD.

METHOD SIX.

Monotonous Tones.—Final Hypnosis.—Fixation of Gaze.—Convergent Strabismus.

The method in common use at the University of Nancy, France, is as follows: The subject is comfortably seated in an easy chair, with his back to the light, and the operator stands by his side, holding up two fingers of his right hand about twelve inches from the subject's eyes. The subject is told to look intently at these two fingers, and, as far as possible, to keep his mind a blank, as soon as the eyes begin to show symptoms of weariness the Hypnotist begins in a low monotonous tone of voice to suggest sleep as in Method One.

Sometimes the operator without waiting for these symptoms to appear will start at once, telling the subject, "You are beginning to feel drowsy; your eyelids are quivering; your eyes are getting tired; sleep is coming," until gradually the condition of the subject diverges more and more from the normal. The final Hypnosis generally comes suddenly. The eyes close quickly, deep breathing takes place, and subject is sound asleep. You can now proceed to induce Suggested Catalepsy and Somnambulism or Trance condition, as given in Method One. Hypnosis is induced by this method by fixation of gaze, combined with suggestion. The strained position of the eyes, and the slight convergent strabismus which results, produces a tired condition of the brain, and causes sleep, four or five minutes generally sufficing to develop complete Hypnosis. (This being a psychological explanation for those who wish it.) The exact object held before the subject's eyes matters little. It may be the operator's fingers, or a disc held before the subject about a foot from the eyes, placed in such a position that when looking at it the gaze will be strained upward, it being absolutely necessary that the subject concentrate his mind and whole attention as well as his eyes on the object, and think only of watching the object held in the operator's hand.

CHAPTER IX.

POST-HYPNOTIC SUGGESTIONS.

Interesting Phenomena—Designated Place, Time or Date.—No Knowledge or Realization.—Cigarette Fiends.—Drunkards.—Strange Hypnotic Power.—Altered Personality.—Indelibly Impressed.—Good Results.

In all deep stages of Hypnosis, the characteristic phenomena of post-hypnotic suggestions may be obtained. These phenomena are very interesting, and can be used to good advantage in curing disease and evil habits, and consists of giving a suggestion while the subject is in the Hypnotic sleep, to be carried out after he has again been brought back to his normal condition.

It is not necessary to its success that these suggestions should take effect immediately. Post-hypnotic suggestions can be given to take effect at any designated place, hour, or date, or any set future time. As an illustration, give a subject a post-hypnotic suggestion while he is asleep, to the effect that to-morrow at one p. m. he will come to your house or will go to sleep at any hour stated, and he will most certainly do so.

Any suggestion or command given during Hypnosis will take effect post-hypnotically, if properly made when the subject is in deep Hypnosis or sound asleep and under the control of the operator, or susceptible to suggestion.

It is possible to obtain the fulfillment of post-hypnotic suggestion at an extremely distant date. Suggest to a subject while he is sound asleep that in eight weeks he will mail you a letter with a blank piece of note paper inside, and during the intervening period you may yourself forget the occurrence, but, in exactly eight weeks, he will carry out the suggestions. Suggestions of this nature are always carried out, especially when the suggestion is to take effect on some certain day or date named. Suggest to a subject that in ninety days from a given date he will come to your house with his coat on inside out, and he will most certainly do so.

One strange part of these phenomena is that when awakened after post-hypnotic suggestions have been given the subject has no knowledge or recollection that he has been given any suggestions, and thinks that his acts are due to the natural course of events.

To set one person against another and cause

him to hate the other, induce deep Hypnosis in the regular way and suggest to him that Mr. B. has done him a great wrong or injury, and that when you wake him he will hate and despise Mr. B. When he wakes up he will have no knowledge of what you have done with him or how you have changed his condition of mind toward Mr. B., but he will have no friendship for Mr. B., that can be depended upon. Take a drunkard or a cigarette fiend and give him suggestions that when you wake him up the sight or smell of whiskey or cigarettes will make him deathly sick and that if he tries to take a drink of liquor or smoke a cigarette he will get so sick that he can not stand up, then awaken him and have someone offer him a drink or a cigarette and he will refuse, giving as the only reason that the sight of them makes him sick. The writer has cured some of the worst cigarette fiends by this method when nothing else would cure or affect them. The Hypnotist can by this method and strange Hypnotic power change the personality of an individual, and mold his character to suit his wishes, but he should hesitate in employing it for purposes otherwise than beneficial, as he is liable to place the subject in a very unhappy position, and of course be responsible for evil results.

As stated above, it is absolutely necessary when giving Post-Hypnotic suggestions that the subject should be sound asleep and deeply under the Hypnotic influence.

Then take a position beside the subject and while giving the suggestions make passes over the subject's forehead and give suggestions in a firm and decided manner. Repeat them over several times so that they will become indelibly impressed upon the sleeper's mind, and, when through giving the suggestions, to have good results. Wake the subject up instantly, but give suggestions before doing so, that he will have no memory or recollection of your having given them after you have awakened him.

CHAPTER X.

ANAESTHESIA, HOW PRODUCED.

Suspended Animation.—Complete Anaesthesia.—Positive Suggestions.—Hat and Needle Tests.—Public Demonstrations.—Singing with Sewed Tongues.—Minute Inspection Allowed.

In all deep stages of Hypnosis anaesthesia can be produced in any part of the human body, animation being entirely suspended and all sense of feeling or pain removed from that particular part of the body.

To produce complete anaesthesia for hat pin tests or surgical operations, decided suggestions must be given while the subject is in deep Hypnosis, that he has no sense of feeling whatever in that particular part on which you wish to operate upon.

The proper way to put a hat pin through the cheek is first to immerse the pin in some good antiseptic solution. Then give positive suggestions that he has no feeling in his cheek, that that part of his face is completely insensible to pain, and that he will not feel the least pain when you put the pin through. Then take any ordinary steel hat pin and force it through his cheek, and he will not feel any pain, nor will blood flow when it is withdrawn.

If you wish to put a needle or hat pin through the tongue of a subject have him extend his tongue as far as possible, then take hold of it with a handkerchief and give decided suggestions that he has no feeling whatever in his tongue, and that he cannot feel any pain in his tongue.

While giving public demonstrations on the stage the author has often sewed three or four subjects' tongues together and while thus fastened had them all sing or dance. They of course having no knowledge of the sewing process, for the author would sew one subject's tongue to his ear, and put two or three hat pins through the tongue or cheek of another subject, and let them pass through the audience for minute inspection. Where this was done, using citizens who had come upon the stage so that all doubt and idea of fraud or simulation would quickly vanish.

It must be understood, however, that the subject for these tests must be down in a very deep stage of Hypnosis and the suggestions must be given in a decided and convincing manner, that he has no feeling whatever in his tongue or

ANÆSTHESIS

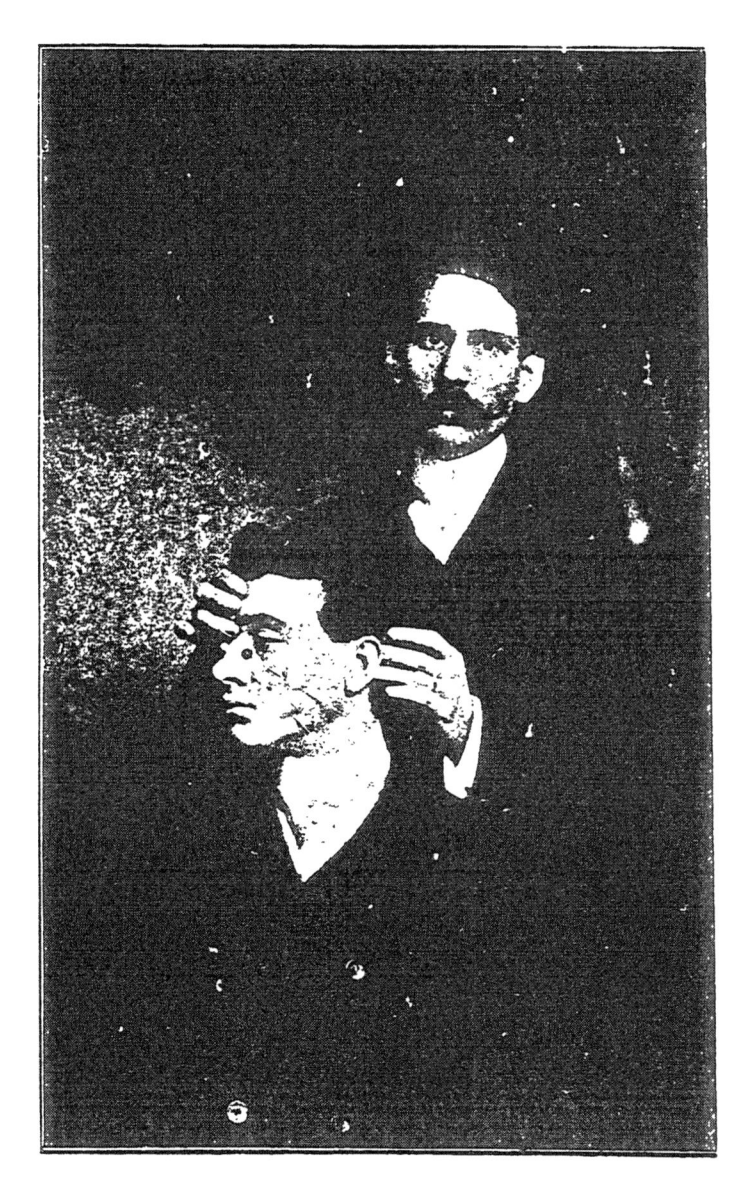

cheek. When this is done, you need have no fear of hurting the subject, for he will not feel the least pain, providing you have done your part properly.

CHAPTER XI.

CATALEPTIC OR RIGID STATE.

Marvelous Demonstrations.—Wonderful Weight Sustained.—Stone Breaking Tests.—Caution Necessary.

The author has during his long experience as an operator given some marvelous tests of the Cataleptic or Rigid state.

While giving private demonstrations for the benefit of some physicians and other professional men in a certain Ohio town, a young lady quite tall was used as a subject, for the Cataleptic test, her weight being but 120 pounds, as I afterwards learned. She was put in the Cataleptic state, her body becoming rigid as a bar of iron. While in this condition, her head was placed upon the back of a high dining-room chair, and her feet upon another. In this position her body sustained without apparent effort four hundred and five pounds, the combined weight of three persons who stood upon her body while in this position. No ill effects resulted, the young lady stating that she had no knowledge or recollection, after being brought out of the condition, of what had been done with her while Hypnotized.

The stone-breaking tests with which nearly all are familiar, is where a stone weighing between five and six hundred pounds, is broken with a sledge-hammer, while lying on the breast of a young man whose body is Cataleptic, with his head resting upon one chair and his feet upon the back of another. These are demonstrations and tests which appeal to one's common sense and reason, and no person, who has ever witnessed these phenomena, doubts their authenticity, especially if is extended to him the privilege of handling the sledge.

CATALEPTIC STATE—HOW INDUCED.

In this state the subject's body becomes perfectly rigid.

The following instruction should be strictly followed: Have the subject stand perfectly firm upon the floor, arms straight down by his side. Inform him in a decided manner that you are going to make every part of his body rigid. Then place the two middle fingers of the right hand upon the back of his neck, pressing the spine, the same fingers of the left hand on the back above the hips, also pressing the spine.

Then in a deep, decided voice say: "Rigid, rigid, rigid; every part of your body is getting rigid, rigid, rigid."

Then stroke the arms and limbs downward, and make passes from the head down, slightly touching the body, all the while keeping your mind and will intensely concentrated upon the subject. Hold the thought firmly in your mind that he is and will get rigid.

When his body has become rigid, take him by the shoulder and have an assistant take hold of his feet. Place his head upon the back of one chair and his feet upon another. His rigid body will hold up one or two persons' weight quite easily.

CAUTION.—Do not keep the subject in the Cataleptic state too long. Awaken him by clapping your hands at the side of his head and loudly saying, "All right; wake up," after he has been placed upon his feet again.

CHAPTER XII.

LETHARGIC OR INDEPENDENT STATE.

Lethargic Condition Dangerous.—Bishop the Mind Reader.—Unmistakable Signs of Life.

The Lethargic state is an independent condition next to death, in which the subject ceases to have any connection with the operator, having passed out of his control. It is caused by the operator letting his subject sit inactive too long after he has induced somnambulism or trance. This is a very dangerous state and the operator should guard against it by keeping the subject interested and doing something, for if left to himself and preoccupied he is very liable to pass into this state.

If you have more than one under control at the same time, keep them all busy doing something to engage their attention. If you cannot use them all, wake some of them up before they pass into this apparently lifeless condition.

There is no doubt but that Bishop, the mind-reader, was in this condition when the autopsy was performed upon his supposed dead body, as his heart and other vitals gave unmistakable signs of life.

CHAPTER XIII.

CLAIRVOYANT OR SECOND SIGHT.

Seeing at a Distance.—Stolen Articles Found.—Murders and Thieves.—Suspension of Physical Senses.—Lifeless Body.—Independent Action of the Mind.—Mediating Sense Organs.—Clairvoyant Phenomena.—Ability of Clairvoyant Subject.—Psychic Organism.—No Possibility of Fraud.—Severe Tests.—Deepest Stages Best.—Hindoos of India.—Accurate Account of Distant Battles.—Occult Phenomena.—Intellectual Advancement.—Mind Invisible and Immaterial.

Clairvoyance, or seeing at a distance whereby a person can be put into a trance so that they can locate lost, hidden, or stolen articles, ferret out murders, thieves, etc., is possible when this condition is properly induced and a good Clairvoyant subject used.

While in this condition the human mind has the ability to extend its faculties of conception far into space. The condition consists of an absolute suspension of the physical sense organs, the body appearing almost lifeless, or as if in a deep sleep. The ordinary way of perceiving through the sense organs is for the time interrupted and an independent action of the soul or mind takes place.

This action is an immediate perceiving of things, conditions, and persons as they actually and really exist in their very nature, and not as they appear to us, often hypercritically through mediating sense organs, as clairvoyance is finer and farther reaching than the sight of our dull eyes.

Before giving specific instructions for producing the Clairvoyant state, I will give the reader a description of some of the phenomena of this trancelike condition and the ability of some of those whom I have had in the Clairvoyant state. The mind of a good Clairvoyant subject can be made to leave the body, so to speak, and be directed to any given locality anywhere in space, and can give an intelligent and accurate account of things being done at that particular place. It matters not whether it is in the same room, or a mile, or one thousand miles away, the mind will find the spot. Distance makes no difference because the human mind or the psychic organism of man does not recognize space.

One evening while giving some demonstrations at a social gathering in the city of Cleveland, Ohio, I was asked to try some clairvoyant work and selected a subject from among those present, fortunately securing an excellent one. Among the tests, was one that barred all possibility of guess work or fraud. The subject was a young man of about 24 years of age, and, after being put into the Clairvoyant state, he was securely blindfolded by two young gentlemen who took all necessary and unnecessary precautions to prevent their friend (not mine) from deceiving them to accommodate me, a stranger to them all.

When all was ready one of the young ladies present was asked to go to the library and select any book she wished and go to another room, shut the door, and sit down ostensibly to read the book selected.

The test seemed a severe one, especially with a new subject, and means of verification on the spot. I was then requested to ask the subject where the young lady had gone? He unhesitatingly replied that she was in a certain room in the house, naming the location of the room upon being asked to do so. When asked what she was doing he stated that she was sitting down reading, and then proceeded to give the name of the book and number of the page where the book was opened by the young lady.

All of these answers, upon investigation, were found to be correct. The subject could tell the number of any person's watch, while in this condition, which was more than some of the owner's themselves knew. He also told of things that were occurring in another part of the city, which were afterward found to be correct. In all of these tests given, there was not the least possibility of mind reading or telepathy entering into the tests, as I myself was ignorant of the knowledge procured by the young man while in the Clairvoyant state, therefore he could not have received it from my mind.

Nobody excepting the young lady herself knew the number of the page where she had the book open, yet he answered this question as readily as any of the others. All Hypnotic subjects do not as a rule make good Clairvoyants, and a person should be selected for this kind of work who is of a quiet and sensible disposition and can be put into a very deep stage of Hypnosis. These qualifications are absolutely necessary if good results are obtained.

Always put the subject asleep as in Method One, using the Mesmeric passes, and when the subject is in a deep, sound sleep state to him that he has now entered the Clairvoyant state and condition, and that while in this condition his mind has the ability and power to leave his body and go anywhere in space that you may direct it. Deeply impress this fact upon his mind, and keep him down deep asleep by giving suggestions while he is being blindfolded, then ask him if he is ready to go to any designated place. If he answers in the affirmative you can proceed to direct his mind to any place or locality you wish, and, if you have him deep enough under the influence, he will in a few minutes answer any question regarding the place or person.

It is a common thing for the Hindoos of India to self-induce this condition, giving accurate accounts of battles going on miles away. This fact is well known by all familiar with India and her people, who are well advanced and Adepts in Occult Science. If human testimony is of any worth, there is abundant evidence reaching from the remotest ages to the present time, and is as unimpeachable as is to be found in support of any fact or thing, that the human mind has the ability, when the proper conditions are provided, to leave the physical body and go where directed in space.

We are now stepping into a new era. The future will mark the closing of this century as one of intellectual advancement in Psychic and Spiritualistic science. The century now opening is the era of interesting study and the advancement of the science of the human mind or soul of man. Every observing and intelligent person is anxious to learn more of the mind, that mysterious immaterial and invisible part of man. Those who interest themselves in the study of Hypnotism and Mesmerism will be amply rewarded.

CHAPTER XIV.

HYPNOSIS SELF-INDUCED

Human Possibilities.—Material and Immaterial Forces.—Occult Phenomena.—Natural Laws.—Voluntary Hypnosis.—Dormant Powers.—Auto Suggestion.—Removing Pain.—Power of Suggestion Over Disease.—Vital Forces.—Recorded Results.—Apparent Death.—Self Hypnotization.—India Fakirs in the Far East.—Famous Holy Man.—Sealed Coffin.—Revived After Six Weeks Apparent Death.—The Sceptical Rajah.—Medical Details of Occult Phenomena.—Dr. McGregor.—Eye Witness to Disinterment.—Organs and Functions of Body Controlled.—Suspended Animation.—Killed by Suggestion.—Dr. Hack Tuck.—Condemned Frenchman.—Disease and Kindred States Produced by Auto Suggestion.—Morbid Suggestions.—Possibilities and Susceptibilities of the Human Mind.

That Self-Hypnotization lies within the limit of human possibilities is an established fact. And this possibility becomes greater when we realize that everything in this wonderful world which consists of material and immaterial forces combined is based upon common sense and reason.

All Occult phenomena, whether Psychic or Spiritualistic, is the result of natural laws. Nothing ever happened but that which is due to facts, circumstances and conditions.

It most certainly is a wise provision of nature for anyone to be able voluntarily to place himself in the Hypnotic state. He who can by an effort of his will enter the Hypnotic condition is complete master over his own mind or soul.

"He that ruleth his soul is mightier than he that taketh a city."—(Prov. 16:32.)

"He that hath no rule over his own spirit is like a city that is broken down, and without walls."—(Prov. 25:28.)

These powers lie dormant in all mankind and can be easily developed by the proper application of the will, or what is known as auto or self-suggestion, combined with concentration. The author has often self-induced this condition, and by auto-suggestion is able to remain asleep any desired length of time or make any part of his body insensible to pain. He has repeatedly removed pain from different parts of his body by concentrating his mind upon the affected parts with the absolute determination and desire of removing the pain.

This psychological fact demonstrates the power and effect of suggestion, either auto or spoken, on disease and pain, for when by the proper suggestions we place the psychic forces on the defensive against pain, disease, and death, with the intention of driving them out of our body, we invite and receive in their place health and strength. But when these lines of life forces are weakened by adverse suggestions disease enters the body at that point where exists the greatest deficiency of vital force.

To be able properly to induce this condition the psychic powers must be developed in the following manner: The beginner should go into a quiet room and lie down in a comfortable position, and with the concentration of the mind and sight upon some small article or object in the room, let the body become perfectly relaxed. Take in slow regular breaths, holding the thought and idea in the mind (exclusive of all other thoughts) that every breath you draw is putting you sound asleep, and that you are becoming totally unconscious of your surroundings.

It is absolutely necessary that you concentrate the mind and whole attention as well as the eyes upon the object and think only of going sound asleep, and that you will remain sound asleep for an hour, two hours, or any reasonable length of time desired.

When self-inducing the Hypnotic sleep, a certain time or hour to wake up should be decided upon and this time fixed in the mind. At the expiration of this self-appointed time you will wake up feeling greatly refreshed and strengthened.

These are auto-suggestions and can be given to suit the convenience of the sleeper, who may if he so desires remain in the Hypnotic sleep for almost any length of time.

Recorded results show cases where the Hindoos of India have self-induced the Hypnotic condition and remained in that state for six months, animation being entirely suspended, so that no signs of life could be detected.

There are many authenticated cases known of apparent death being produced by self-Hypnotization or auto-suggestions, accomplished by India Fakirs and other religious enthusiasts in the far East. One remarkable, and I believe thoroughly well-authenticated instance, is of a famous holy man, who, to demonstrate his ability to some distinguished men and convince the Maharajah Runjeet Singh that he possessed this power over his psychic organism, apparently died and was placed in a sealed coffin, which was put in a vault, the entrance to which was also sealed, and closely guarded by soldiers. At the end of six weeks, the time set by himself, the coffin was carried out of the sepulcher in the presence of the Rajah and several credible witnesses, English as well as native, and when the coffin was opened, his body had every appearance of death. But, after being slowly revived by his faithful servant, the ghastly-looking and corpselike being raised up in his coffin and addressed his first words to the sceptical Rajah, saying, "Do you believe me now?"

Full medical details of this phenomena are given by Dr. McGregor, who was an eye-witness to the disinterment, in his "History of the Sikhs."

There are many other well-authenticated cases of vivi-sepulture known, whose genuineness can not be questioned.

There is another case similar to this in some respects, the truthfulness to which the author can testify. A young man who, by practice, has acquired the power of being able to enter the Hypnotic sleep at will, can awaken at any set time. To effect this he has only to lie down and concentrate his attention on sleep, and retain the thought in his mind that he will awaken after a certain length of time.

He is also able to apply auto-suggestion as a curative and can relieve himself of any abnormal condition. By this means he has remarkable control over the organs and functions of his body, as was demonstrated to the entire satisfaction of two physicians and myself, who were present to witness the experiment and satisfy themselves whether or not it were possible for a human being by an effort of his will to suspend animation and then, as it were, come back to life again. Upon examination by the physicians before entering the state, his pulse and heart were found to be perfectly normal; and, after stating that he would remain self-hypnotized an hour, he lay down and became perfectly still and composed, one of the doctors holding his right hand while the other held a mirror to his mouth.

In less than a minute his pulse began to sink gradually until pulsation ceased, as did all action of the heart, while not the least soil of breath was discernible on the mirror.

The physicians, after a close examination, could not discover the least sign or symptom of life, and his body had every appearance of a corpse, animation having been completely and absolutely suspended, continuing so for an hour.

Then the pulse and heart slowly and gradually again resumed their normal condition, as did the lungs and other viscera.

It is unnecessary to state that the doctors were greatly surprised, and insisted upon an examination after he had resumed the normal condition, but failed to detect any harmful results.

The power and effect of suggestion on the imagination is wonderful, and there is no question but that sickness and even death itself is often caused by suggestion, as is readily seen in an instance given by Dr. Hack Tuck.

The victim was a Frenchman, who had been condemned to death for committing some crime, and his friends, wishing to avoid the disgrace of a public execution, consented to his being made the subject of an experiment. It was stated to the condemned man that it had been decreed that he must be bled to death. The executor then bandaged the victim's eyes, and, after his arm had been slightly pricked, a small stream of warm water was made to trickle down it and drop into a basin, the assistants all the while keeping up a continuous comment on his supposed weakening condition. "See how pale he looks. He is getting faint, his heart is beating slower and slower, his pulse is almost stopped," with numerous other remarks of this sort. In a short while the miserable man died with decided symptoms of cardiac syncope from a hemorrhage, without having really lost a single drop of blood, a victim of suggestion.

That decease and kindred states are induced

by auto-suggestion and can likewise be induced by suggestions from without, there is no doubt.

Let a man's friends repeatedly tell him that he is looking bad, and that he does not seem able to be about, that he should take care of himself, or he will be down sick with this or that complaint, and it is almost a certainty that he will temporarily deteriorate in health.

As in the case of the farmer who was given suggestion of this sort, for a joke. After being assured by a number of persons that he looked bad and was not able to be around, really did take to his bed and went through an unmistakable attack of fever. Although he was in good health previous to the suggestions given him. This of course was a wrong and unwarrantable joke, yet these same effects are often produced by well-meaning persons, who have the habit of always commiserating their friends and acquaintances for not looking well.

"Disease can be, and is, caused by morbid suggestion, either auto or spoken."

"Disease can be, and is, cured by healthful suggestions, either auto or spoken."

This is an indisputable fact known to all advanced thinkers who have a scientific knowledge of the nature, possibilities and susceptibilities of the human mind or soul of man.

CHAPTER XV.

TO HYPNOTIZE BY TELEGRAPH, TELEPHONE OR MAIL.

Subtle and Mysterious Influence.—Irresistible Power.—Professional Operators.—Sleep Induced by Telephone.—Sedate Individuals Made to Dance and Sing Without Their Knowledge.

That a person can be affected and influenced while conversing with the operator over the telephone, either long-distance or local, or Hypnotized by a telegram or letter sent by the Hypnotist who may be miles away in another city, is one of the strange characteristics of Hypnotic influence, but nevertheless a true one, as can be quickly demonstrated by any one who understands the proper modus operandi.

And startling as it may seem, the person influenced in this manner has not the remotest idea that the message or letter he receives is the means of conveying to him the subtle and mysterious influence of Hypnotism, or that he is already at the time of receiving the communication under the influence of the Hypnotist, who has by a few well applied suggestions at some opportune time, placed him within the mysterious and irresistible power of Hypnotism. The method or means by which this is accomplished is known only to a few professional operators, and by its use can be produced some marvelous results. Your audience will attribute it to the strange Hypnotic or Mesmeric power you possess. It is brought about entirely by the use of Post-Hypnotic suggestion. When you have a subject or friend deeply under the influence and dead asleep, say to him, "If I ever call you up by 'phone and say to you, you are getting sleepy, a sleepy, drowsy influence is coming over you, sleep, sound asleep, you will instantly become sleepy and go sound asleep standing at the 'phone, and will stay asleep until I wake you up." He will most certainly go to sleep standing at the 'phone, but should be seated in a chair by friends until you come and awaken him.

To Hypnotize a person by telegraph or mail, give Post-Hypnotic suggestions, that, if you send him a message on Monday, either by wire or mail, informing him that to him the following day will be Sunday and that when he awakens next morning he will know and realize that it is Sunday.

He will without fail arise next morning with

the impression that it is Sunday, and if in the habit of attending services, dress and go to church at the accustomed time, and will not hesitate to inquire why the church is locked, and will insist that it is Sunday morning.

Take a very sedate individual and after giving suggestions in the proper manner, send him a letter saying that at four p. m. on the following day he will start to dance and sing. He will at the designated hour, no matter where he is or what he is doing, commence to dance and sing, greatly to the astonishment and horror of his friends.

CHAPTER XVI.

PEOPLE HYPNOTIZED AGAINST THEIR WILL.

Hypnotized at any Future Time.—Shrewd Hypnotist.—
Utter Helplessness.—Operator Master.

A great deal has been said for and against any method or system of Hypnotizing anybody against their will, especially if they have never been previously operated upon. I will first give instructions for Hypnotizing against the will by the use of Post-Hypnotic suggestion.

After you have once Hypnotized a person say to him that you can now Hypnotize him at any future time, that you can put him to sleep whenever you wish, that he has no power or ability to resist you, and you can Hypnotize him against his will or wish any time you please. Of course if a person has never been under the influence, you cannot use Post-Hypnotic suggestions to influence him against his will, but there is a way in which a shrewd Hypnotist can succeed in putting people under the influence who really do not care to be hypnotized.

No method by which a person who has never been a subject can be Hypnotized against their will has ever been given to the public. But be that as it may, the author has during his years of experience discovered and successfully used a method by which he has succeeded in Hypnotizing a great many people against their will, who had never been operated upon before, which if strictly followed will succeed. It requires an extraordinary amount of determination upon the part of the operator to overcome the resistance of the person who does not wish to be put asleep.

This method will be found useful at parties or gatherings where you may have some difficulty in procuring subjects if nobody present cares to be Hypnotized, and you can't get a willing subject, politely ask some member of the party to let you give him or her a simple test with their hands, saying it is nothing but a slight test and will not do any harm or hurt anybody. A little talk along these lines will invariably induce someone present to allow you to try their hands. Then proceed to fasten the hands of the individual who just intends to let you try, as he thinks. After you have fastened his hands tightly let him struggle, but keep his eye, and after he is satisfied that you have him fast, release his hands in the regular way; then put his hands together a second time. Of course it is understood he does not intend to let you put him to sleep and make him perform before his friends. That is his idea at least. And he doesn't intend that you shall if he can prevent you. When putting his hands together the second time, while you are giving the suggestions, hold his eyes steady and strong until you get him dazed. You can detect the dull stare coming in them, and when this is pronounced and an expression of utter helplessness takes the place of the smile that may have been on his face when he sat down, suggest to him in a determined tone of voice that he cannot move or leave the chair, that every part of his body is paralyzed, and he will know by the fierce gleam in your eyes that you are master. You can then proceed by a few well-chosen suggestions to put him dead asleep and induce somnambulism or trance in the regular way. He will ever afterwards be your subject if you understand your business in giving Post-Hypnotic suggestions.

CHAPTER XVII.

INSTANTLY HYPNOTIZED.

Instantaneous Hypnotism for Public Demonstrations.—At the Opera House.—Hypnotized by a Finger.—Marvelous Effects.

Hypnotizing instantaneously is generally used in the show business when giving public demonstrations, but of course can be used by any operator. A person can be instantly hypnotized, either on the street, in a crowd, or while seated in an opera house, by a wave of the Hypnotist's hand, by his having previously given Post-Hypnotic suggestions to this effect.

Suggest to a number of subjects when you have them on the stage that whenever you point your finger at them or pass your hand in front of their face they will fall asleep. When you have a subject asleep, suggest to him that if he is in a crowd, or on the street and you catch his eye or look at him he will become instantly hypnotized and will follow you anywhere.

Of course the subject has no knowledge that you have previously implanted this irresistible influence in his psychic composition, neither has the public, and the absence of this knowledge will cause the effects to be considered more marvelous by your friends and the public.

Cannot Close their Mouths. Hypnotized young men at the command of Prof. DeLaurence are unable to close their mouths, though they are plainly trying to do so.

CHAPTER XVIII.

HINDOO SLEEP, HOW INDUCED.

Fakirs and Adepts of India.—Monotonous Music.—Peculiar Sensations of Hindoo Sleep.—Suggestive Position of Operator.—Completely Fascinated by Hindooism.—Rotary Motion of the Body.—Concentration. Universal.—Amusing Incident of Hindoo Sleep.—The Conceited Gentleman.—Hindooism Contagious.—Complete Humiliation.—Cake Walk.—Good Drawing Card.

This method or manner of inducing Hypnosis receives its name from the Hindoos of India, where it is universally used by the Fakirs and Adepts of that country, who to facilitate the induction, use as an accompaniment some monotonous music.

The Hindoo sleep is principally used in this country by professional showmen, who from the stage can succeed in putting a number of persons asleep while sitting in their seats in different parts of the opera house.

People who have entered the Hindoo sleep give accounts of being conscious of a peculiar drawing sensation while the condition is being induced. These sensations from the description given of them are evidently caused by the suggestive position assumed by the operator while inducing the Hindoo sleep.

One subject in particular relates that the arms and entire body feel as if some power or influence were drawing them up, and that just before the final Hypnosis is induced his arms felt as if they were about two inches long. Other subjects tell of similar experiences and symptoms.

To the close observer the expression on the face of a person while the Hindoo sleep is being induced is decidedly interesting, some subjects appearing as if completely fascinated and possessed of the idea that their body is really paralyzed. This frozen expression can be removed, however, by suggestion after the subject becomes sound asleep, the countenance assuming a contented and peaceful expression if the proper suggestions are given.

When wishing to induce the Hindoo sleep, the operator should sit upon the floor, with his legs crossed and drawn up something after the manner of a tailor, then after placing the thumb and little finger of either hand together at their tips, he should begin a slow rotary motion with his body, but that part of the body below his hips should remain perfectly motionless.

This rotary motion can be successfully accomplished by a little practice upon the part of the operator. During this operation the eyes of the Hypnotist should be concentrated upon those of the person whom he wishes to put asleep. The operator can take his position any desired distance from the subject, who should be sitting in a comfortable chair.

When operating from the stage the Hypnotist should sit in the center of the forward part of the stage, and during the movements of his body should cast his eyes over the entire audience, with no individual concentration, but by his will must influence everybody present, or as many as possible. This should be kept up for about ten or fifteen minutes and at the end of that time a good operator will probably have quite a number of persons sleeping in their seats in different parts of the opera house.

If desiring music as an accompaniment a low monotonous tune may be played from an organ or a melodeon, which are best for this purpose. While the operator is inducing the Hindoo sleep he should remain silent as only mental suggestion is given, and when operating from the stage he should, after having induced the sleep in a number of persons, come from the stage and awaken all of them individually, but before doing so it is better to give suggestions to the effect that they will be all right, and then nobody will feel any of the drawing sensations before spoken of, after being awakened.

The number of people that can be simultaneously affected or influenced in this manner depends of course upon the ability of the operator and the size of his audience.

There happened during a public demonstration given by the author in one of the Eastern states quite an amusing incident.

Among the earlier arrivals at the opera house one evening was a young gentleman accompanied by two of his lady friends. He stated in a positive and decided manner to those around him that nobody could hypnotize him, and that he would be there when I put him asleep and made a fool out of him. I apparently paid no attention to this conceited fellow during that part of the show preceding the Hindoo sleep. But when the time came for inducing it I gave him and his two friends a considerable of my attention, which amount I am sure was sufficient.

Shortly after beginning to induce the Hindoo sleep the young lady sitting at his right side showed decided symptoms of sleepiness, and directly her head sank over and she went sound asleep, whereupon the young gentleman gallantly placed his hand under her head, with the intention of resting it, which was just what I desired him to do. By this time the other young lady sitting at his left became afflicted in the same manner, she also going sound asleep, and the young man supported her head also with his left hand, much to the amusement of those whose attention had been attracted. I then proceeded to give the young gentleman whose hands were already filled with trouble, an individual but slow and sure application of Hindooism.

The expression upon his face was interesting in the extreme; and I think but for his former statement that he would be there when I put him asleep he would certainly have attempted to leave the opera house, for in his eyes before they closed in sleep could be seen a look which was meant as an appeal to save him the humiliation of being put asleep after such positive statements upon his part, that this could not be accomplished.

After waking up his lady friends and some others who were sleeping, I took the young fellow upon the stage and had him do a cake walk and chase an imaginary flock of bees from his flowing locks. It is unnecessary to state that he was the whole show from then on, for, being a young man of considerable importance in the city where he resided, he caused roars of laughter by such actions as fishing in an imaginary stream from the edge of the stage, using a broom stick for a pole, and going among the audience soliciting shoes to shine.

Scores of the egotistical young man's friends came every night during the balance of the week to see him perform, for being well known and a splendid subject, he was a good drawing card.

CHAPTER XIX.

SYMPTOMS OF HYPNOSIS.

The final induction of Hypnosis is generally preceded by a decided contraction of the pupils of the eye, they then dilate, and remain largely dilated until the normal condition is again assumed.

There is also noticeable a marked quivering of the eyelids. These vibrations are often continued for some time after the eyes have closed in sleep. In all deep Hypnosis the eyeballs turn upward and remain in that position until the subject is awakened or opens his eyes during somnambulism.

CHAPTER XX.

THE DIFFERENT STAGES OF HYPNOSIS.

Important Classifications Necessary.—Attempts at Classifications.—Unsatisfactory Classifications.—Prof. Bernheim.—Detailed Classification.

The depth to which each subject enters Hypnosis varies with each individual; but there are certain classifications which are important, as some pass into a light sleep, others into a deep sleep; this depends upon the susceptibility of the subject to Hypnosis and the ability of the operator.

As a rule the Hypnotic sleep deepens with every Hypnosis till about the fifth or sixth induction; by this time the subject has usually reached his deepest stage.

These different stages or degrees of Hypnosis vary from a condition which only an expert Hypnotist can detect as Hypnosis, to a state in which strikingly abnormal conditions are present. The variety of stages are many and different observers have made attempts to classify them. These various classifications are, however, extremely unsatisfactory, no two agreeing, their divisions being from two up to ten, which latter view is held by Prof. Bernheim.

It would be a waste of time to dwell upon the different opinions thus advanced, and it is useless to attempt a more detailed classification than those given here:

1. Light Hypnosis.
2. Deep Hypnosis.
3. Profound Hypnosis.
4. Somnambulistic state.
5. Cataleptic state.
6. Clairvoyant state.
7. Lethargic state (dangerous).

Profound Hypnosis—No memory on returning to the normal condition of anything that had been said or done while in the Hypnotic condition.

CHAPTER XXI.

HOW TO WAKE A SUBJECT.

No apprehension need ever be felt by the practical operator who has been properly instructed, about having any difficulty in getting a subject out of Hypnosis, or awakening him from the Hypnotic or Mesmeric sleep, for when the proper suggestions, which are an important part of Hypnotism, have been given when the subject is asleep, he will wake up instantly when told to do so by the operator.

No case is known where an operator, who understood his business, and had confidence in his ability as an Hypnotist, has ever had the least difficulty or trouble in waking a subject. Where this has occurred it was due to ignorance on the part of the operator, who had not been properly instructed.

After Hypnosis has been induced and the subject is sound asleep give him decided suggestions that when you count three he will wake up, that he cannot remain asleep but will have to wake up immediately. Then awaken him by counting three, and saying in a loud voice, "All right; wake up," and he will be wide awake. The operator should never lose his presence of mind or become excited if a subject does not wake up when told to do so, but should in a confidential manner repeat the suggestions and make him wake up by loudly saying, "All right now."

CHAPTER XXII.

CURING DISEASE BY HYPNOTISM AND SUGGESTION.

Long Words and Ominous Sentences.—Suggestive Therapeutics.—Materia Medica.—Nervous Diseases.

The physician who attempts to frighten his patients by telling them that bad results follow the induction of Hypnosis is beginning to be generally recognized as one using long words and ominous sentences wherewith to cloak his own ignorance; for, as everyone with a knowledge of the true principles of Hypnotism knows, great benefit and good are to be derived by its use. The physicians and surgeons who have a knowledge of Hypnotism and are combining Suggestive Therapeutics (which is the treatment of disease by Hypnotism and Suggestion) with the present method of practicing, are fast outstripping their slower brothers who are depending wholly upon their learning of physiology and Materia Medica as the only means of combating disease.

This is a mistake, and the physician who does not consider a knowledge of psychology as necessary and of as much importance in treating his patients and curing disease as is physiology, is as ignorant of the origin, action and cure of disease as he is of the science of being.

All diseases and especially those of a nervous origin can be entirely cured, while the patient is quietly engaged enjoying a peaceful sleep, from which he will awaken free from pain and greatly relieved in mind and body. When desiring to treat any person, always induce the sleep by the Mesmeric passes as given in Method One and when you have the patient in a sound, quiet sleep give suggestions to the effect that when you wake him up he will be entirely free from all pain, and that when he goes to bed at night he will go sound asleep and have a good night's rest and will feel greatly rested and improved in the morning.

The suggestions should be given of course to suit the individual case you are treating, the operator using his best judgment. And after treating a few cases he will have no trouble in relieving all in whom he has induced the sleep.

CHAPTER XXIII.

PERSONAL MAGNETISM.

Magnetic Personality.—Power of Fascination.—Agreeable Personality.—Disagreeable Characteristics.—Don Quixote.—Decidedly Unpopular.—Honesty Best.

To those who wish to acquire that peculiar magnetic personality which gives charm of manner and power of fascination that is sure to win and retain the respect and admiration of those with whom you meet and associate with through life, particular attention must be given to their personality and an effort should be made to cultivate an agreeable personality.

It always pays to be pleasant. Nobody is as unpopular as a disagreeable person, or one of an aggressive disposition. We all have certain disagreeable characteristics in our nature; these should be eradicated by close thought and attention upon our part. During conversation avoid arguments by all means and never contradict anybody. Make this a rule above all others. If you are urged to announce an opinion, do it rather by asking questions, as if for information or by suggesting doubts. When anyone expresses an opinion which is not yours you must know that he has as much right to his opinion as you have to yours, and why should you question it?

His error does you no injury, so why should you become a Don Quixote and try to bring all men by force to one opinion? If a fact be misstated it is possible he is gratified by a belief of it, and you have no right to attempt to deprive him of the gratification. If he wants information he will ask for it, then give it to him in measured terms; and, if he still believes his own story and shows an inclination or desire to dispute the fact with you, hear him and say nothing.

It is his affair, not yours, if he prefers error, and you should let him keep it and not make yourself decidedly unpopular by trying to get it from him. Make a special study of the characteristics of those you wish to impress favorably, and while conversing with them, always look them straight in the eye; do not stare, but cultivate a steady gaze, always holding their eye while you are talking, and with your will impress them with the fact that you are telling a truth and mean what you say, as it always pays to be honest. The eyes are the windows of the soul of man, and as he reckoneth in his heart so he is.

A man with an honest heart always has a truthful expression in his eyes, and people will have confidence and trust in him, which is essential to success in life and business.

CHAPTER XXIV.

HYPNOTISM AND CRIME.

Dangers of Hypnotism.—Religious Views.—Criminal Events.—Moral Nature.—Criminal Suggestion.—Judges and Lawyers.—Criminal Assaults.—Hypnotism, Ether and Chloroform.—False Pleas.—Criminal Reports.—Fatal Syncope.

In considering the danger to which the public is liable from a criminal or improper use of Hypnotism, we must dismiss from our minds as far as possible the popular ideas with regard to the subject.

The playwright and the novelist have both apparently been at pains to write the greatest amount of nonsense in the shortest possible space, and they have been at liberty to write with no knowledge and little understanding, since the public who listen to and read their productions care little and know less. It would be a waste of time to discuss the various fallacies which underlie this class of writing. Suffice it to say that no work of this character with which the author is acquainted gives any true idea of the Hypnotic state or the dangers which may attend its use.

The members of the medical profession who

have attacked the use of Hypnotism have shown very little acquaintance with the subject; their views appear to be religious rather than scientific, and it is unnecessary to discuss opinions which are not based upon scientific observation.

The dangers of Hypnotism are, I believe, often exaggerated, but there is probably no question but that it can be used for evil purposes, and that by criminal suggestion a person can be made to commit crime.

Recent criminal events which are supposed to have been caused by Hypnotism have been the means of bringing the question of the employment of Hypnotism for criminal purposes prominently before the legal and medical professions, with the object of finding out to what extent it can be used to aid crime.

Different opinions have been advanced as to whether or not it is possible by the means of Hypnotism to make a person commit a crime or an act that is against their moral nature.

There are many who claim that this cannot be done, while others maintain that in Hypnotism there is a power which will give one person such absolute control over another, as to insure the accomplishment of crimes without exposing themselves, but of course a belief either way does not prove the truth or falsity of the question.

I believe that the question should be met with perfect frankness, and think that by all means judges and lawyers should closely study the possibilities of Hypnotism as an aid to crime.

There is scarcely any doubt but that criminal assaults may be committed with no subsequent recollection of the occurrence. But why should this be made a contention against the use of Hypnotism, when we have exactly analogous abuses of ether, chloroform, and many other drugs?

Every person when Hypnotized acts out his or her own individuality, and if the wish and desire to do right and avoid crime and evil is strongly grounded in a man's soul, or an essential part of his individuality it is not probable that suggestion would cause him to so widely depart from these principles as to commit an evil act, or crime, any more than would the pertinacious solicitations of friends cause a sincerely temperate man to take a drink of liquor.

And I assume that a false plea of having acted under Hypnotic influence is a much more probable event than the perpetration of crime by its use. If the contention against a universal knowledge of Hypnotism being given to the people is because it possibly may be used for criminal assault, the same contention should be made against the use of chloroform, as criminal reports and records show that it has, and can be used for criminal assault. And in the face of this fact it must be acknowledged that there is less danger of criminal assault by the use of Hypnotism, than there is from drugs, because it is not everybody that is so susceptible to Hypnotic influence as to become anaesthetic, while everybody becomes anaesthetic and amnesic under the influence of drugs.

It is not to be supposed that well-meaning people will object to a spread of the knowledge of Hypnotism because of this contention.

It is my opinion, and also my experience, that the power in every human being for good is more potent than that for evil, and that it would be very much harder to make the good man do wrong than influence the bad man for good.

From my observation and experience I think it safe to state that the possibilities of Hypnotism being used for criminal purposes are very remote.

For, supposing that a Hypnotist did get absolute control over a subject and rendered him so sensitive to his suggestions that he could induce him to commit thefts and other crimes, and at the same time be unconscious of the promptings or influence which had impelled him to commit the act. Could not the subject of this criminal suggestion be re-hypnotized by another operator and made to disclose the name of the one who had hypnotized him for criminal purposes and intent? For all enlightened men know that if a subject is hypnotized a second time he will remember all the suggestions which have been made and all the events which took place during the previous Hypnosis, but on awakening he will have no recollection or knowledge of these events. Still, in the hands of an expert Hypnotist, it is difficult to place any definite limitations on the reaction of a subject to criminal suggestion, as he might commit a crime from their effects. It would also be comparatively easy for the Hypnotist to kill his subject, with no lesion to be found post-mortem.

In good subjects the heart-beat can be modified to a remarkable degree by suggestion, and a continuation of skillful suggestion might produce a fatal syncope; again, suggestion may be made by the Hypnotist in his own interest against those of the subject.

Of course it is important that every one should recognize that the dangers of Hypnotism when used by the ignorant, the unscrupulous, or the malicious, are real and not imaginary. Although it would be nonsensical to attack Hypnotism itself, because like every other agency it is open to abuse, the person who is going to be hypnotized has a right to demand that he have some guarantee that the qualifications of the Hypnotist and his good faith and honor are unquestionable.

CHAPTER XXV.

HYPNOTISM AND INSANITY.

Attracting the Insane.—Border-Land of Insanity.—Morphine, Opium, Cigarettes and Narcotics.—Enslaving Habits.—Mental Habits.—Mental Faculties, Wrecked and Ruined.

Every one who has ever had anything to do with the insane, knows how difficult it is to get them to fix their attention on anything except their delusion for any length of time, but after gaining an influence over them they can often be greatly benefited and cured.

Cases of this sort, however, are of rare occurrence and until some mechanical contrivance can be invented for attracting their attention and holding it long enough to induce Hypnosis, there is not much that can be done in the direction of helping these unfortunate people out of their miserable condition.

There is, however, an extensive field for the use of Hypnotism in that borderland of insanity occupied by dipsomania.

There are to be found a great many persons who are on the verge of insanity by the excessive use of morphine, opium, cigarettes and numerous other narcotics.

In cases of this kind Hypnotism and suggestion are found to be very powerful agents, and can be made the means whereby the unfortunate victim of these habits is enabled to take his first step towards reformation and cure.

The morphine and opium habit can be successfully treated by Hypnotism and suggestion, it usually taking about ten or twelve days to effect a permanent cure.

When these habits are cured by Hypnotism there is an absence of that distressing mental anguish and suffering which is always felt when these enslaving habits are quickly broken off by other means.

Persons who are addicted to the use of these narcotics usually enter a deep state of Hypnosis, sometimes at the very first induction. When decided suggestion is given to those who use narcotics or stimulants that they can and will sleep and rest without their use, it has the desired effect.

One pitiful case cured by the author was that of a young lady who had become addicted to the use of morphine by its having been prescribed by a young physician, for a very painful injury.

When her parents, who were quite wealthy,

accidentally discovered that their daughter was using this terrible drug, they refused to give her money with which to purchase it.

After vainly trying to sleep and being unable to receive any rest for two nights, she became desperate and sold her diamond ring, a gift from her mother, to buy morphine with.

She received her first treatment during the forenoon, with decided suggestions that upon retiring that night she would immediately drop into a sound, quiet sleep and not awaken until eight o'clock the next morning. These suggestions were carried out, and in two weeks she was permanently cured of all desire for the drug.

The cigarette habit, which quite often causes insanity, can be broken in this manner, as can masturbation, which can be cured by Hypnotism and suggestion when all other remedies and means fail, as these are mental habits. A continuation of them will rack and ruin the mental faculties. Drugs cannot cure these habits as drugs have no mental effect.

CHAPTER XXVI.

HYPNOTIZING ANIMALS.

Diverse Organizations.—India Fakirs and Aissouans.—Venemous Snakes Handled.—Continuous Stimulation.—Strange Eggs Hatched.—Professional Horse Trainers.—Timid Mind.—Fearless Mind.—Animals Simulate Death

That the hypnotization of animals and snakes is possible to a limited extent, has been demonstrated in various ways, by experiences on animals of such diverse organizations that there is scarcely any question of its being within the limit of possibilities, especially by the Fakirs and the Aissouans of India, who are reported to be able, by the use of music, to so charm and fascinate the most venomous snakes that they are rendered perfectly harmless, and that these snake-charmers can induce the snakes while in this condition to closely imitate the snake-charmer's movements.

The author has frequently induced a state of Catalepsy (if this may be considered an accurate term for the condition induced) in rabbits, frogs, guinea pigs and fowls, by a monotonous continuous stimulation. And while in this condition they would remain perfectly motionless and unresponsive to ordinary stimulation.

This state can be best induced by firmly fixing them in one position for three or four minutes and then quietly removing the restraining influence, and it will be found that the animals will remain in this position, however abnormal, for quite a length of time. Experiments of this kind is a well illustrated example of hypnotic influence in animals.

Another interesting experiment of this sort is to draw a chalk line and hold a chicken with its beak on this line, and it will be found that the creature will remain in this fixed position for several minutes.

The method of changing the nest of a setting hen, which is familiar to most farmers, owes its success to Hypnotism. The way this is done is to hold firmly the fowl's head under its wing for a few minutes, and then rock it slowly to and fro, with the result that it apparently goes to sleep. While in this condition it can be removed to another nest, or from one nest to another, and seems to have no realization of the change. It will contentedly remain sitting upon the strange eggs until they are hatched.

A dog may be rendered docile and obedient by

the means of a fixed look, and will seldom attack a person if looked straight in the eye.

The tiger always endeavors a rear attack to avoid this look, and there is scarcely an animal, but that can be kept in check if not allowed to escape the eye of the person attacked.

Many animals self-induce Hypnosis by simulating death the moment they are disturbed by falling into a state of complete insensibility, but apparently recover as soon as the cause of their alarm is removed.

Professional horse trainers evidently owe their exceptional control of unmanageable horses to something akin to Hypnotism.

One favorite plan used by expert horse trainers is to look the horse straight in the eye, all the while giving their own head a rotary movement similar to that used for inducing the Hindoo sleep. In a few minutes the unruly horse becomes perfectly obedient, greatly fearing him who has by this peculiar process become its complete master.

That the condition of mind maintained by a person while around or handling a horse influence it and has considerable to do toward governing the horse's actions, there is little doubt. A man with a fearless mind and not afraid of horses will pass them in safety, while one with a timid mind and afraid of those dangerous parts (his heels) will unhesitatingly be kicked skyward.

Everybody is familiar with the fact that snakes often charm birds and frogs, fixing them so they cannot move, when they then become the easy prey of the murderous reptile.

An interesting story is related of a woman in Northern Ohio, who one day while washing some clothes was Hypnotized by a large snake. When found by her friends she had become so charmed and fascinated by the snake that her body was rigid and immovable. Wondering what had caused the trouble one of the party who happened to glance upon the ground discovered a snake. After the snake was killed the woman again regained consciousness.

CHAPTER XXVII.

HYPNOTIZING BY A ROTATING MIRROR.

A mirror is sometimes used in hospitals when it is desired to Hypnotize a large number of patients at once. It consists of four small mirrors, fastened upon cross pieces which when set in motion rapidly revolve, and is termed the rotary mirror.

Some people, it is found, by gazing at this instrument become Hypnotized at once, and by its means a whole roomful of people can be Hypnotized in a very short space of time.

Another curious little instrument which is said to be now employed altogether for inducing Hypnosis at the famous Charcot clinic in Paris, France, consists, I am told, of a plain black rubber cylinder about four inches long and an inch and a half in diameter. In it is a little revolving disk, set flush with the surface and about the size of a silver quarter.

This disk is divided into four segments, two of which are dead black and two white, and it is set into rapid motion by pressing a button connected with some coiled springs inside.

It is said the operator stands in front of the subject who is to be Hypnotized, and holds the curious little instrument about three inches from a point midway between the brows.

The patient is then told to concentrate his mind and gaze upon the little wheel, something slightly fatiguing for the reason that it throws the eyes a trifle out of focus. In about four or five seconds the button is pressed and the disk is set in silent motion. The swift whirling of the disk brings about the degree of concentration necessary as a preliminary to producing Hypnosis, and is said scarcely ever to fail.

The mind is momentarily emptied, so to speak, of any other thought or idea, and is in a condition highly susceptible to suggestion.

CHAPTER XXVIII.

MIND AND BODY; OR THE SCIENCE OF BEING.

Sorrow and Gloom.—Origin and Cause of Disease.—Mental Forces.—Science and Art of Living.—Problem of Disease.—Pure Thoughts.—Bodily Imperfections.—Thoughts Entertained and Maintained.—Parental Individuality.—Sea of Life.—Hereditary and Environments.—External Impressions.—Impure Thoughts.—Afflictions and Misery.—Cause and Effect.—Premature Grave.—Unwelcome Guest.—Morbid Tendencies.—Hosts of Good and Evil.—Fate, Ambition and Revenge.—Tragic Deeps of Earthly Life.—Mental Impressions.—Narcosis.—Disappointment and Gloom.—Fear and Expectancy.

"As a man thinketh in his heart, so he is."
(Prov. 23:7.)

We all must know that every human being prefers health and happiness to disease and misery, and that sorrow and gloom are but the result of mistakes. When we look with pity upon those around us, upon their pain and poverty, their sorrow and despair, we realize the truth of Shakespeare's words, who was great and good enough to say:

"There is no darkness but ignorance."

It is only ignorance of the origin and cause of disease and pain, that makes sickness and misery so prevalent.

Many persons are loud in their lamentations and wonder why God has sent these afflictions upon them, while they bring them upon themselves, by an improper use of their mind, or mental forces.

This is the great fundamental error of existence and the cause of all disease, sorrow and despair, as very few have any true knowledge of the science and art of living.

The puzzling and perplexing problem of disease finds its only rational solution in the relation that exists between mind and body.

The question is often asked why so many souls pass out of the physical body through the agency of disease? Why is it that you so seldom hear of a natural death? Why so few persons have a perfectly sound and normal body?

There is but one logical answer, the human body is developed and strengthened by the mind or soul within. And good, pure healthy thoughts build and make a strong body.

"All that we are, or ever will be;
Is the result of thought."
—DeLaurence.

It is right thinking, or pure thoughts, that give health and happiness; while wrong thinking, or bad thoughts cause bodily imperfections and disease.

No observing or intelligent person will deny that a despondent or gloomy condition of mind affects the health. The body is the outgrowth of the mind, representing the nature and condition of the life forces within it. In the right control and direction of thought, lies the remedy to cure and heal disease and pain, for we must deal with causes, and not effects.

A mind perfectly controlled and directed in the proper channels of strength and health giving thoughts, will produce and maintain a normal healthy body.

The human mind is a loom—constantly weaving. Our thoughts are the warp and woof of that fabric the mind weaves, which composes and builds our body. If the thoughts out of which the fabric has been woven are good, pure and health-giving thoughts, we have a strong healthy body, free from disease and pain; but if our thoughts are gloomy, or evil, and impure, then our body which is the fabric woven from this impure and defective warp and woof, will be afflicted with disease and ailments.

Our Manner of Thinking.—The thoughts that

are entertained and maintained in the mind or soul, shape and form the destiny of man.

Bringing to him sickness or health, poverty or wealth, afflictions or happiness, and takes him either to Heaven or Hell.

All that we are, or ever will be, is the result of what has been thought, either by ourselves or our mothers. The mother by her condition of mind molds and forms the characteristics and traits of her child.

Children are always stamped with parental individuality. Therefore every one sails this great sea of life, which is composed of mind, destiny, and will, in a bark formed of two substances,—hereditary, and environments. Our surroundings from which we receive external impressions, or suggestions, furnish us with thought material. If we receive into our heart or soul, good material for pure health-giving thoughts, we have strong healthy bodies. If we accept or select that which is bad, and makes impure and evil thoughts, we have weak and diseased bodies, and are surrounded by afflictions and misery.

"And he said, that which cometh out of a man, that defileth the man."—(Mark 7:20.)

The right control and direction of thought is whereby the soul receives health and happiness.

Thought influences, builds and controls every organ and function of the physical body.

Mental discouragements and depressions are accompanied by disinclination for exertion and a sense of bodily fatigue.

A combination of symptoms and complaints follow disappointments and worry, and the removal of the cause is followed by an immediate removal of the effect.

A depressed or wearied condition of mind, inhibits life and energy, and a constant dwelling of thought on some real or imaginary trouble, wrecks the mind and destroys the human body. While worry sends to a premature grave or the insane asylum all who welcome or accept it as a constant companion. The extent to which it kills is appalling to contemplate, and we should drive it out of our mind as we would a thief or an unwelcome guest from our house.

It is the duty of every man to suppress his evil and morbid tendencies, and encourage and develop those that are good and noble.

For bad is he, indeed, who is possessed of no good qualities. We all must know that in every human soul, as in the smallest bud or flower, are encamped the opposed hosts of good and evil, of disease and health, over which flow all the tides and waves of destiny and will, over which sweep all the storms of fate, ambition, and revenge, upon which settle the gloom and darkness of despair and death, and all the sunlight of content and love.

Every human soul at birth is launched upon the mighty sea of right and wrong, of disease and health, of joy and grief, of life and death.

And it is only by the knowledge of the science of being that we are able to avoid the rocks and tragic deeps of earthly life.

Physical disease and discomfort are always traceable to mental causes, and are mental in origin, as the material body always responds to mental impressions.

There is an abundance of evidence reaching from the remotest ages to the present time, to support or demonstrate this fact.

"A merry heart doeth good like a medicine,
But a broken spirit drieth the bones."
—(Prov. 17:22.)

A quiet, pleasant and composed condition of mind maintains a healthy body.

"Sleep knits up the raveled sleeve of care."
—DeLaurence.

Joy and happiness do the system far more good than drugs. Narcosis (sleep produced by narcotics) leaves the system depleted and weakened. While the sleep of those with a peaceful and contented mind restores and builds up the wasted energies of the body.

Disappointment and gloom fills the physical body with disease and pain, sapping life's vitality and energy.

Hatred and revenge poison the blood and he who entertains revengeful thoughts brings a curse on himself.

Anxiety and fear, or an irritable condition of mind, brings on hysteria, insomnia and other nervous diseases.

Those who are confident in their ability to ward off disease and sickness, thereby placing the life forces on the defensive against its entrance into their system, can expose themselves to contagious diseases without any fear of contracting them.

This is especially true of professional nurses and physicians who are so accustomed to being among the sick that they naturally have no fear of exposing themselves to the most contagious disease.

It is this fear and expectancy of taking a disease, and which fills the mind of most people when they enter a sick room, or are in any way exposed, that invites disease and makes the body susceptible by weakening its forces, which, if properly governed, will throw off the most contagious disease known.

"For the thing which I greatly feared is come upon me, and that which I was afraid of is come unto me."—(Job 3:25.)

CHAPTER XXIX.

TELEPATHY, MIND READING AND SPIRITUALISM.

Transmission of Thought.—Inherent Power.—Physical Senses. — Telepathy. — Thought Transference. — Mind Reading.— Psychic Forces.— Subconscious Mind.—Mental Impressions.—Psychic Organism.—Independent Action.—Sense-Perception.— Psychic Action.—Material Forces.—Second Sight.—Simultaneous Action.— Material World.— Mind Upon Mind.—Intense Concentration.—Deep Emotions.—Mentally Agitated.—Suspension of Physical Senses.—Clairaudience.—Trance.—Psychic Activity.—Impressions and Influences.—Physical Laws.—Chemical Decomposition.—Death.—Evolution.—Soul and Body.—Condition of Existence.—Cause of Existence.—Departed Spirits.—Birth to Death.—Psychic and Material Forces.—Natural Laws.—Psychological Conditions.—Spiritualistic Phenomena.—Manifestations and Communications.—Immortality.—Departed Souls.— God's Universe.—Premonition of Death.—Agent and Recipient.—Thought Vibrations.—Thought Influences.—Clairvoyants, Mediums and Mind Readers.— Guilty Conscience.— Influences Transmitted.— Love and Devotion.

Telepathy is the transmission or communication of thought from one mind to another, by an inherent power in all mankind, which enables him to transmit or communicate his thoughts or ideas to another independent of the physical sense organs.

These phenomena, accurately speaking, are called Telepathy, but are also known as Mental Suggestion, Thought Transference, Mental Impression and Mind Reading.

This power, which lies dormant in each of us, is an action of the mind or psychic forces, which many designate as the soul, subjective or subconscious mind of man, and by which he is able to communicate or perceive mental impressions, thoughts, and influences, independent of the ordinary or objective means of communication.

The physical sense organs are the mediums by which and through which the mind or psychic organism externalizes itself, and also the means by which the human mind receives external knowledge and impressions.

These sense organs or mediums transmit and express the thoughts, desires, emotions, and wishes of the soul or mind of man.

They also convey to the mind within the body knowledge, influences, impressions and intelligence from without.

Telepathy is the communication or transmission of thought or the peculiar and actual condition of one mind to another independent of, and without the use of, these physical senses.

This transmission or sense-perception is most successful during an absolute suspension of these mediums or physical sense organs.

The fact of mental impressions, modifications, telepathy and all near and distant action of the psychic forces is known to all familiar with the well known laws which regulate psychic action.

The soul or mind of man, which is his actual existence, consists of an organism of psychic forces externalizing itself in and through the physical organism of material forces which constitute the human body.

These two stand in the same relation to each other as thought and the expression of thought.

Now when this psychological view and fact is applied to the subject, it must be readily seen that for these psychic forces there exists no space; and that the success of telepathy (psychic action) does not depend upon nearness of space but upon the proper psychic relations which must exist between the agent's and the recipient's mind. When these conditions have been conformed to, it matters not whether they be in the same room or thousands of miles apart, the result is the same.

It is a well known and established fact that by a willing, a strong desire and concentration of mind in the agent directed toward the recipient that thought transference, or telepathy, takes place. This demonstrates that there is no distance in space between two minds.

This is known to be a fact, not only in the transmission of thought and the process of mesmerizing but also in those singular cases of second-sight and of reading the past, present, and future of another mind.

All of this clearly demonstrates that the success or result of these phenomena depends upon actual psychological conditions of the mind and is entirely independent of space, which is an attribute of the corporeal world. It being clearly a spaceless action of mind upon mind, as the psychic forces are spaceless and, therefore, entirely independent of external extension.

These forces act where they are and yet apparently on corresponding forces far away in space, because for them there exists no space. There being a simultaneous action of forces upon forces, or mind upon mind, no matter where these forces are stationed in the material world or space.

The psychic organism or forces are not confined in and by space, as they always act wherever and whenever they find corresponding psychic forces to be acted upon.

Thus acts the human mind or soul which is

an organism of psychic forces, and is most certainly a spaceless action of mind upon mind, while the mind or soul has its abode in the physical body.

Phantasms, apparitions and all psychic and spiritualistic phenomena are clearly the action of a purely psychic nature, of one psychic organism upon another, and usually takes place when a person is in great danger or otherwise mentally agitated and has his mind fixed upon some distant relative or person.

The sudden coming into consciousness of an absent friend or relative who personally appears soon after proves the action of the human mind or psychic forces at a distance and their immediate action where willed by intense concentration of the mind or soul; for when by strong desire and deep emotions, the mind, that is, the entire psychic organism, becomes so mentally agitated that the ordinary way or means of perceiving through the medium or instrumentality of the bodily organs or physical senses is for the time interrupted (the physical senses being entirely suspended) and an independent action of the psychic forces, or mind (Clairaudience), takes place instead.

Every one can understand why in this state (trance) the body apparently becomes almost lifeless, or as if in a deep sleep, and upon the other hand, why this psychic activity intensely concentrated upon another mind or person is capable of communicating or transmitting thoughts, impressions, or an influence to another, there being an immediate effect and action of forces upon forces, and not, as a great many think, of mind upon matter, as this action is entirely independent and separate from the physical body.

For what has the body to do with that action— a body cannot, nor does not, act at a distance, so all observing people must consider it entirely the action of the soul or mind, as the human mind during normal health is a substantial psychic organism, and most certainly has action independent of the body.

The human soul is an organism of psychic, and not of material forces, and as such lies absolutely out of the range of mechanical and chemical analysis and consequently also beyond the grasp of the physical laws of dissolution, and therefore cannot fall a victim to chemical decomposition. Therefore what follows after death, that is, after the separation of soul and body? The soul is still subjected to the laws and conditions of evolution, for when the soul abandons the body it merely changes a condition which is

THE CATALEPTIC STATE.

no longer of use for its progress or future evolution.

The cause remains all the same, the psychic forces or soul continue in their action, which is an immediate perceiving of things as they really and actually exist, and not as they appear through mediating physical sense organs.

Death is simply a change in the condition of existence, but does not affect in the least the cause of the existence, any more than it does its activity; and therefore it may be assumed and asserted that departed spirits (the souls of men) continue to exist after so-called death. Every observing person will admit that the soul constantly increases in internal strength and intelligence from birth to death.

Many may ask by what right do I assume that the soul has a continual and immortal existence after it abandons the body, in the society of which it is no longer able to increase its powers and consequently unable to make any further progress?

Our personality is not lost by bodily death. We shall not be formless and disembodied shadows. For we cannot die. Paul says: "Although the outer man perish, the inner is renewed day by day," suggesting the existence of an imperishable soul or spirit within the human body.

Why the simple fact of the soul's continued increase and growth in strength up to its departure from the body. It is then that man dies not because life (the vital power of soul) leaves him, but because the soul departs from the body, but by no means ceases to exist.

This assumption is in accord with the nature of the soul of man and the laws by which its psychic and material forces combine.

Taking this psychological view of the action of the soul or mind of man, which is the result of natural laws while the soul inhabits the body, and whose psychic action is entirely independent of the physical body, when the normal senses are suspended, it is no violent assumption to assume that the mind or soul of man can when the proper psychological conditions have been provided, receive and send mental suggestions or communications independent of the physical senses or body, and that the human soul when it becomes an immortal spirit by having passed out of the body should, and does sustain the same relation and psychic action toward the mind of mortal man, after its becoming an immortal spirit that it did while an inhabitant of the body.

That the mind of man is susceptible and can be influenced or receive a communication from an immortal spirit or soul which has passed out of the body is a fact known to all having a good and true knowledge of spiritualistic phenomena.

There is plenty of human testimony that the souls of the dead do return, manifestation and spirit communications come to us in our highest and purest condition of mind.

It is then that the soul asserts its immortality. This evidence demonstrates that the human mind or soul can and does exist without the physical brain or body, and is an intelligence still, when disconnected from the material body.

This furnishes proof of a future life for which so many crave, and for want of which so many live and die in anxious doubt, so many in positive disbelief.

Every human heart hungers for the presence and return of the dear departed. They come to us, we feel their presence, realize their influences, yet we heed them not, due to ignorance of the science of the human mind or soul.

Possibly external and scientific proof of all this phenomena cannot always be readily secured on the minute, but can the mind of man be measured with a rule, or a human soul weighed in a balance. or seen and dissected under a microscope?

The wise philosophy of some of our most sapient scientists is inadequate in things pertaining to the human heart or soul, and their ominous head-wagging over facts it will not account for, certainly looks foolish to intelligent and discerning people.

They accomplish much good work in their way, but they cannot dissect the human mind or soul of man, or measure God's universe.

Most every person will acknowledge that Telepathy or thought transference independent of the normal senses is possible. To support this fact plenty of evidence can be obtained by any observing person.

For instance, let some terrible accident happen to a distant relative or friend, who is far away, and we receive a premonition or mental impression of the very facts of the case. Many persons have been heard to remark that they had a warning or impression that some near or loved one was sick and in danger.

Now many people have got up in the morning after an almost sleepless night, to receive bad news of some sort. They say, "I knew it. I felt something was wrong." Plenty of evidence and similar cases of this kind can be found.

One case among others which have come under the author's notice was that of a lady residing over two hundred miles from her sister, who, when last heard from, was enjoying her usual good health. Upon retiring one night at her accustomed bed time, she went to sleep as usual, but was awakened about two a. m. by, as she supposed the voice of her sister calling her. She heard her sister call her twice by her given name, and got up, supposing she had come unexpectedly during the night, and went to the door with the intention of admitting her, but found no one there.

This greatly puzzled her, for as she stated afterwards she was positive of being wide awake when her name was called the second time, and that she recognized her sister's voice. The next morning at seven o'clock she received a telegram stating that her sister had died unexpectedly and alone, between two and three a. m., of heart trouble.

This, strictly speaking, was what is termed Clairaudience, and was caused or brought about by the intense desire of the stricken one to see and speak to her sister before she died. Realizing as she did that she was dying, her mind became so deeply agitated and was so strongly concentrated upon her distant sister that she received this warning or premonition of death.

Two persons will often simultaneously express the same thoughts or ideas in the same words, or one will say I was thinking of that very same thing myself.

Many times we think or speak of some person whom we have not expected, and, coincident with our thoughts, they appear at the door.

As stated before, distance does not make any essential difference in the transmission of thought, only as to the extent it is taken into consideration by the agents or recipients, who if they lack confidence of their ability to project their thoughts to remote places away in space and to receive such communications and intelligence as might seem possible if the agent and recipient were not so far apart, will not be successful.

Confidence is absolutely necessary, and distance or space must not be taken into consideration at all, for as much as it is considered, just that much will it detract from the ability of the one who entertains these adverse ideas.

The mind is directed into space by confidence and belief; without this confidence the mind will hesitate and accomplish nothing.

The agent, or transmitter, is the one who desires to impress the mind of another at a distance.

The recipient is the person who receives a

mental impression or suggestion from the mind of another.

It is absolutely necessary that the recipient let his mind become passive, and as far as possible hold his physical or objective senses in complete abeyance, so that he may be the more readily impressed and receive the communications from the sender.

The transmitter, or agent, upon his part must concentrate his mind and keep it upon any particular object, thought, or impression he wishes to project to the recipient.

No special mental effort is necessary to transmit or convey these thoughts or impressions. The agent should concentrate and compose his mind upon what he wishes to convey, and think intently of it, and the effect will be transmitted to the mind of the recipient.

The success of thought transference depends upon the vividness and ability of the sender to picture in his imagination any selected object, thought, or impression he wishes to transmit to the recipient, and the ability of the recipient to become passive, letting his mind become quiet and ready to receive any impression, and also to be able to judge correctly what he is desired to receive.

For the new beginner it is best that the distance be not great, and the first few experiments in Telepathy should be tried with the agent in one room and the recipient in another. After the agent has decided upon what he wishes to transmit let him sit down and concentrate his mind as directed above, the recipient of course being in another room.

A few figures will be found best at first, then different objects can be used; these should be followed by transmitting short phrases and words, and in time the distance and amount of information can be enlarged upon.

If wishing to communicate with some person in another city at a distance a certain time should be decided upon for the transmission to take place. The agent and recipient should both make notes of impressions and the names of objects transmitted and received.

To the observing and intelligent person the effect, influence, or action of mind upon mind is instructive and interesting. Much can be learned by observing and noting the different effects and results of these psychic forces both in public and private life.

Go into an opera house, church, or public hall and concentrate your mind upon some certain person sitting in front of you, and if your concentration is perfect the person will invariably turn and look at you unconscious of course, that you had intentionally made him turn his head or influenced and willed him to do so.

Most every one has noticed the many impressions and thought influences that vibrate between two persons when shaking hands for the first time. These vibrations are especially pronounced if each has his eye fastened upon the other.

Again, on going into a dark room where some person is concealed, and quiet, his presence is often felt and made known to you by the effect of his mind upon yours as he is thinking of you. Not unlikely his mind is anxious as to his discovery and this anxiety upon his part betrays him to you.

Step up quietly to the bedside of a highly sensitive person who is sound asleep and he immediately becomes aware of your presence, although you have not made an audible sound, and if he does not awaken he will move uneasily in his sleep.

There is scarcely a person who, but some time or another is his life, has not become conscious of being stared at, and people who are especially sensitive in this respect are quite often annoyed and ill at ease if made the object of attention.

It is best if you belong to this class of sensitives to make your mind positive, thereby throwing off these influences and not permitting them to annoy you. This can be done by assuming a determined condition of mind, as man should always meet man with an honest, decided and steady gaze. No clairvoyant, trance-medium, or mind reader can fathom the positive mind, while a passive or uneasy mind is like an open book to those who understand this branch of psychic science. Criminals are often detected in this manner, as their uneasy and guilty condition of mind, of which they are only too self-conscious, surrounds them with an influence which is transmitted to the shrewd officer, or detective, who, when he receives an impression that the man is guilty, shadows him on suspicion, and ultimately arrests the guilty man, his suspicions having been well grounded.

In the elucidation of this subject, I have endeavored to state fairly that there does exist means based upon natural law, by which thoughts, influences and communications can be transmitted to another mind, as well as communications received from those of our loved ones whose souls have passed out of the body; but not out of worldly existence—for it is clear we cannot deny the possibility of departed spirits acting upon material as well as immaterial forces in this wonderful world, which consists of material and immaterial forces combined.

This possibility becomes greater when we think of, and realize the many bonds and strong ties of love and devotion which fasten the dear departed to what they have left behind, and which assures their nearness, presence, wishes and desires, to act upon what they loved and left at death.

CHAPTER XXX.

MAGNETIC HEALING.

Miraculous Cures.—Boy Phenomenon.—Magnetic Force, or Personal Magnetism.—Valuable and Worthless Opinions.—Natural Gift.—Miraculous or Superhuman Power.—Vital Forces.—Forces Medicatrices.—Physical and Moral Qualifications.—Methods and Processes.—Fundamental Principles.

"And these signs shall follow them that believe; They shall lay their hands upon the sick, and they shall recover"—(Mark 16:17, 18).

Within the last few years the attention of the public has been attracted by a great many people being cured by what is generally known as magnetic healing.

And in all parts of the country people are practicing it and I think it quite safe to state that many persons have been cured by this means after they had been placed upon the list of incurables. The seemingly miraculous cures made by the so-called Boy Phenomenon and others who have startled the community at different points by performing their cures in opera houses and public halls, have been the means of placing before the eyes of the public evidence which has astonished many intelligent and observing people, and caused them to hesitate before they condemned this manner of healing the sick as a humbug.

There are a great many people who have considerable doubt as to the existence of any such thing as magnetic forces or personal magnetism, or that when the hands of a healthy person are placed upon the body of a sick person that there can be transmitted any influence or power which heals disease or removes pain.

When persons say that they do not believe in this, or that, or that they do not believe certain things can be done, it should make little difference to the man who has as much right to investigate these things for himself as others have to express an opinion.

No person's view or opinion should be accepted for more than it is worth. Opinions or views are valued as is everything else, according to their composition, or the material from which they are molded or made. The person who has had an opportunity to observe and make scientific investigations upon some certain subject, certainly has an opinion more valuable than one who has formed individual ideas in an egotistical and ignorant manner, and composed of limited views and observation. Every man, before he accepts an opinion or view manufactured by another, who may have been incompetent, has a perfect right to seek the best obtainable or refuse all advanced and investigate for himself.

The world is full of people who are always ready to express themselves upon every subject, and the less their opportunity for scientific investigation upon any one point the greater is their desire to relieve themselves of their hastily formed ideas.

Such people are, in the first place, not competent to render an opinion, else they would not offer gratuitous ones.

Magnetic healing as is everything else in occult science, or pertaining to the human mind, based upon natural law, and magnetic healing, or the power to heal and cure disease, is not a natural gift, which a few favored ones possess, but is a gift common to all mankind.

Every living person has this power, if shown how to develop it and use it to the best advantage of themselves and others.

Any person of ordinary intelligence and good physical health, can become a magnetic healer. He need not necessarily be supposed to possess any miraculous or superhuman power or be endowed with an over supply of magnetism. To heal or cure an afflicted person by what is termed personal magnetism, simply consists of the proper direction and application of the vital forces, which every living person possesses. As an illustration: let any person place the thumb and fore-finger of the right hand upon the head of another person, at the base of the brain, the same fingers of the left hand upon the front part of the head, above the eyes; keep the fingers in this position, remain perfectly quiet for a short time, and the person will feel the so-called magnetism or magnetic current as it passes from the fingers through their head.

This is the vital force or personal magnetism passing from one person to another. This magnetism, or healing force, can likewise be directed or sent to any part of the human body by making passes or rubbing the body. Whenever an abnormal condition exists in any part of the body and the vital forces or magnetism of a healthy person are applied or directed to that particular part of the body, it removes the abnormal condition by forcing nature or the vital forces to the afflicted parts. Magnetism having for its object the development of what the physicians call the forces medicatrices—that is to say, the seconding of the offices that nature makes to relieve itself, and the facilitating of the cures to which it is disposed—it is essential to act with consonancy in aid of nature, and never oppose it.

Only one sentiment ought to animate the person who attempts to heal in this manner, the desire of doing good to him whose cure he undertakes, and with whom he ought to occupy himself wholly, giving all his attention during the treatment.

This force or magnetism is directed by the will, and belief is necessary to induce the healer to make firm and steady use of the faculties he possesses. Confidence is only the consequence of belief. It differs in this only. Mr. B. believes himself to be endowed with a power whose reality or existence he does not doubt. In order to have good results, or so that the healer may have a beneficial effect upon the person he is treating, there must exist between them a moral and physical sympathy, as there is between all the members of an animated body.

Moral sympathy is established by the desire of doing good to the person who desires to receive it; or by ideas or wishes which occupy them both equally, forming between them a communication of sentiments.

When this sympathy is well established between the healer and his patient then you have provided the proper condition to transmit this healing power or influence.

Thus, the first condition necessary is a steady

will; second, is the confidence which all must have in their own powers; the third is benevolence or the desire of doing good. One of these qualities or conditions may supply the other to a certain degree, but to have effect at the same time energetic and salutary the three conditions must be united.

No Magnetic Healer should undertake to treat a person for whom he feels any repugnance, or if he fears to catch the disease. For to act efficaciously the healer must feel himself drawn towards the person who requires his care or treatment, take an interest in him and have the desire and hope of curing, or at least relieving him.

The power of healing or that of doing good to our fellow beings by the influence of the will, by the communication of the principle that sustains our health and life, being the most delightful, and most precious that God has given to man, he ought to regard the employment of this faculty or power as a religious act which demands the greatest self-collectedness and the greatest purity of intention.

Magnetic Healing or the power to heal disease, is composed of three principles: First, the will to act; second, a sign, the expression of that will; third, confidence in the means employed.

If the desire of doing good be not united to the will to act there will be some effects, but these effects will be unsatisfactory and irregular.

Confidence, which is an essential condition for the healer's mind to be in, is not necessary on the part of the person being treated, as he can have a beneficial effect equally upon those who believe and those who do not believe in Magnetic Healing.

It suffices if the patient yields himself up passively, making no resistance. Nevertheless, confidence contributes to the efficaciousness of Magnetic Healing, as it does to that of most remedies.

The faculty or power to heal disease and cure the sick exists in every human being; but all do not possess it in the same degree. This difference of power to heal in various persons arises from the superiority which some people have over others in moral and physical qualifications. Among the moral qualifications are confidence in one's own power, energy of will, facility in sustaining and concentrating the attention, the sentiment of benevolence which unites us to every suffering being, strength of mind, which enables one to remain calm and collected under all circumstances.

Of physical qualifications, the first is good

health, which gives to us that peculiar power to influence and heal, different from all other known powers or forces of nature, and of which we recognize the existence and degree in ourselves only by the trial and use we make of it.

As this magnetic power or influence emanates from the healer's body and is directed and controlled by an effort of his will, the external organs by which we act are the most proper to convey it with the intention determined by the will. For this reason it is best to use the hands and eyes to heal, and at the same time giving encouraging suggestions as they sometimes produce vital energy and have a beneficial effect upon the mind and body of the patient.

Although the choice of this or that process or method is not essential in order to direct this influence or power, it is best to adopt some certain method and use it habitually without thinking of it, so as to never become embarrassed (thereby detracting the mind and will from the patient) by studying what motion or passes are best.

The processes used by most Magnetic Healers are to approach the sick upon the right side, if convenient, and make passes over the body from the head downward, not touching the body. But in cases of lameness and where the pain is pronounced in any organ or function, the hands should be rubbed or drawn downward over the parts, either outside or under the clothes. For headache draw the hands backward from the middle of the forehead, having the patient close his eyes and remain perfectly quiet.

The faculty or power to heal exists equally and in the same degree in the two sexes; and women can be and ought to be preferred as Magnetic Healers, for women, especially when they require treatment for female troubles.

The observing reader will readily see that the fundamental principles of curing and healing disease, is an application of the life forces or personal magnetism by an effort of the will and a desire to cure or relieve those who are sick and afflicted.

CHAPTER XXXI.

THE PHENOMENA OF HYPNOSIS.

Condition Normal After Hypnosis.—Awakened Instantly.—Apparent Lethargy.—Practical Hypnotist.—Dangers of Experiments.—Ignorant Operators.—Ten Days Sleep.—Various Opinions.—Minimum Average.—Experimental Results.—Princeton or Cornell Students.—Hysterical Conditions.—Different Nationalities.—Recorded Results.—Dr. Liebeault.—Dr. Van Rentezhen.—Dr. Wellenstrand.—Simulation Impossible.—Muscular Contraction.—Rigidity.—Motor Impulses Inhibited.—Ammonia.—Organic Functions Affected.

The condition of a person after being Hypnotized is always found to be perfectly normal, and in the hands of an experienced Hypnotist the subject never finds that he is suffering from any such thing as "drowsiness," or any ill-effects whatever. In fact, great benefit is to be derived, especially by those suffering from nervousness, inability to sleep, etc.

There is never any delay or difficulty in waking a subject, or ending Hypnosis, as in all cases the subject is brought back to the normal condition instantaneously. But in the hands of an unskilled or ignorant operator, however, the subject may pass from the waking state into a condition of apparent lethargy, and out of the control of the experimenter, who is able neither to awaken nor influence his subject. Of course these misfortunes can never occur to the practical Hypnotist.

But the author has known of many such cases, and the danger of experiments in Hypnotism by persons who have never been properly instructed cannot be too strongly insisted upon. When once it is found that the subject does not awaken in obedience to the operator when the proper suggestion has been given, no further effort should be made, but an experienced Hypnotist should be sent for, or, if one cannot be found, the subject should be left alone and allowed to sleep it off.

In the number of cases of the kind which have come under the author's notice, the harm done was almost entirely due to the ignorant and futile attempts made to arouse the subject, whereas if he had been left quietly alone he would have eventually awakened himself.

The duration of the Hypnotic sleep of a subject if not awakened is very variable, and depends upon how deep the subject has entered Hypnosis. If the sleep be light, the subject will often return to the normal state in a very short length of time, but if in a very deep stage, the sleep may continue from thirty to forty-eight hours. Thus an expert operator can keep a person asleep for almost any length of time. The author has been able to keep two subjects asleep for ten days and nights.

Various opinions have been advanced, some well, many ill-informed, with reference to the persons who are not hypnotizable. It would be nonsensical to affirm of any particular disposition or temperament that lends itself to Hypnosis, when we find that over eighty per cent. of all person tried is the minimum average of anyone who properly understands Hypnotism and Mesmerism from a psychological point and in its practical application. Speaking from his own experimental results, the author has found that the class presenting the least difficulties and generally giving satisfactory experimental results is found in young men of average education and of fairly all-round qualities, such a man, for instance, as is a typical Princeton or Cornell student or graduate.

Persons who are very stupid and conceited resemble one another in being difficult subjects. While idiots are not hypnotizable and the insane are excessively difficult to influence. Sex does not appear to materially affect the question, the greater percentage being in favor of men. There is among the physicians a somewhat common misconception prevalent which regards hysterical conditions as likely to indicate easy subjects. Hysteria, or nervousness, however, is as a rule the source of considerable difficulty, and never makes the induction of Hypnosis an easy matter. Nationality has nothing whatever to do with the matter, for taking nationalities of different temperaments there is found scarcely any difference in the recorded results, as the following figures will show:

Out of 1,012 persons tried, Liebault of France hypnotized 985; while Van Rentezhen in Holland hypnotized 169 out of 178 persons, and Dr. Wellenstrand of Sweden hypnotized 701 out of 720 tried. Similar results are given by good operators in this and other countries.

All learned men who understand Hypnotism agree with reference to its medical application that the operator or physican who cannot hypnotize at least eighty per cent. of his subjects or patients is a poor operator, whose opinion is of no value.

Among students and members of colleges and universities the percentage varies from 90 to 94. The author, judging from his observation and experience with a large number of cases, is, on the whole, inclined to regard susceptibility to Hypnosis as generally belonging to men with brains of a good quality; and without question the process of hypnotizing well educated people is easier and takes less time.

In all the deep stages of Hypnosis complete anaesthesia can be produced in any certain part of the body so that the most powerful electric currents can be administered without the patient evincing the least sign of discomfort. Teeth may be extracted or filled and any surgical operation may be performed without knowledge or pain to the patient. The fact that anaesthesia can, by decided suggestions, be produced during Hypnosis in any part of the body, provides the operator with means of demonstrating that there is no pretending or simulation on the part of his subject.

The pulse, respiration, pupil of the eye and temperature can be greatly modified by means of suggestion during Hypnosis. It would be surprising indeed if a condition in which such decided modification of the human organism can be induced could not be of great good from a therapeutic point of view, and many members of the medical profession in this and other countries are using it to great advantage in the treatment of nervous and other diseases.

The extent to which it is possible to obtain muscular contraction is readily observed in the catalepsy of the whole body, when all of the voluntary muscles become absolutely rigid. In this condition the subject may be placed with his head upon the back of one chair and his feet upon another, and his body will remain in a perfectly straight line between these two points.

So complete is the rigidity that the body, while in this position, will sustain an extraordinary weight without giving or bending.

A young lady, by no means athletic or exceptionally strong, while in the Cataleptic state, will sustain with no apparent uneasiness and without any bad results, a weight exceeding a hundred and seventy pounds.

Almost every one is familiar, if only by repute, with the ordinary phenomena of the Hypnotic state. Motor impulses can easily be inhibited and any of the physical sense organs suspended, as deafness and blindness caused. The sense of smell can be suppressed so that thirty-seven per cent ammonia can be held under the nostrils without the subject evincing any sign of inhaling a disagreeable odor.

During deep Hypnosis if the right suggestions

are made the subject will eat pepper under the impression that it is sugar, or he will eat a cake of soap with gusto, with the impression that it is a piece of sweet cake; in fact, every sense and organic function of the physical body can be modified or affected.

CHAPTER XXXII.

THE PSYCHOLOGY OF HYPNOSIS.

Spirit and Matter.—Mind and Matter.—Elements of Hypnotism.— Various Phenomena.— Two Substances.—Proper Route.—Principles Proclaimed.—Confidence and Application.—Natural Laws.—Mind Influences Matter.—System Essential to Success.—Words of Warning.—Action and Reaction.—Public Good.

To attempt to explain Mesmeric or Hypnotic phenomena by the laws of galvanism or electricity, anatomical consideration of the functions of the brain or nervous system, would be very much like explaining vegetation by crystallography.

It is important and essential for learned men and the medical profession to know that the most profound knowledge of the science of physiology will never bring them to the discovery of the theory of Mesmerism or Magnetism. But nevertheless this knowledge will be important and useful to keep the observers from making many errors by enabling them to distinguish what necessarily belongs to Mesmerism and Magnetism and what is due to other causes, by furnishing them with means of verification, and authorizing them to reject all consequences essentially opposite to the well known physical laws. A close study of this work will enable the keen observer to gain a good idea of the phenomena of Hypnotism, Mesmerism and Magnetism, and that man is composed of a physical body, and a spiritual soul, or psychic mind, and that the power or influence he exerts over his fellow men partakes of the properties of both substances.

Hypnotism, Mesmerism, or Animal Magnetism considered as a power or an influence, is decidedly different from all the other powers or forces of nature. It has its natural laws which are not identical with the laws of matter. Considered as a science, it has singular and peculiar principles which cannot be learned, except by close observation, no idea of which can be obtained from other well known sciences, so much I can state with certainty, but I permit myself here to add as an opinion, common with me and many enlightened men, but which I merely propose as an opinion—

That the theory of Hypnotism, Mesmerism and Personal Magnetism is based upon this great principle, that there are in nature two kinds of substances, decidedly different in their

EATING TALLOW CANDLES FOR STICK CANDY.

THE PSYCHOLOGY OF HYPNOSIS.

characteristics and properties—mind and matter: that these two substances act, the one upon the other, but each one possessing laws peculiar to itself.

Among the laws that regulate the action of matter upon matter, many have been successfully brought to light by observation, determined by calculation, and verified by experiment; such are the laws of motion, of attraction, of electricity, of transmission of light, heat, etc. This is not so with the human mind, for although the existence of our soul has been demonstrated and many of its faculties and weaknesses are known to us by observation, its nature is a mystery, for its union with organized matter or the physical body is inconceivable. Many of the psychological laws by which mind affects and acts upon mind are unknown.

Human being are composed of body and soul, act upon, and influence living bodies by the combination of the peculiar properties of these two substances. It is observable that there is in this combined action two separate and distinct elements and a mixed element.

A knowledge of the laws that govern and regulate these two substances constitutes the science of Hypnotism, Mesmerism and Magnetism, and it is only by comparing and closely observing these various phenomena that we arrive at the discovery and the elucidation of their laws.

Therefore it is most certain that those who attempt to establish a theory of Hypnotism, Mesmerism and Magnetism upon properties of matter, or upon physiological views, and those who seek for it wholly in the faculties of the soul, or psychic mind strike equally far from the true theory.

Mesmerism and Personal Magnetism is an emanation from ourselves and directed by volition or an effort of the will, and partakes equally of the two substances, mind and matter, which composes our being, but of course this is not the place to enlarge upon or discuss this subject.

My only object or wish being to teach the science and art of Hypnotism, Mesmerism and Magnetism, and it is more to restrain than to excite those who wish to study this science profoundy, that I have taken the liberty of laying down the proper route they should follow, and the difficulties they must surmount before they arrive at the proper solution or theory.

Further details will be of no especial benefit to the student, therefore I will merely sum up in as brief a manner as possible what has been said in the preceding pages. That for the successful practice of Hypnotism, Mesmerism, Suggestive Therapeutics or Magnetic Healing all that is necessary is the proper mode of application, and confidence.

All of the books which have been published, or theories which have been established since men have acknowledged it as a science, will add nothing essential to the theories or principles proclaimed in this work. What the student needs is a scientific knowledge of his psychic powers and the proper application of them.

To examine into the causes and effects of the different psychic phenomena he must first have acquired by his own experience and observation an entire conviction of the influence and effect of personal magnetism.

Next he should acquire a general knowledge of natural law, then of the psychic organism of man, and its relation to the physical body, and the various conditions in which man is found to exist. Finally he must become acquainted with the effect and influence of the psychic mind upon organized matter, and keenly observe how one man acts upon and influences another by his will or mind.

By following the principles and instructions contained in this book the physician or any person of good physical health and of ordinary intelligence can learn and practice Hypnotism, Mesmerism or Suggestive Therapeutics, either as a means of curing disease or giving demonstrations in Hypnotism or Mesmerism, which is always interesting and amusing.

As system is essential to success in any business, so personal confidence on the part of the operator is absolutely essential to success in Hypnotism or Mesmerism.

Confidence combined with earnestness and a desire to do good, will always bring success.

Hypnotism and Mesmerism can and should be universally used by every one, but the author begs to accompany this statement with the warning, which he always impresses upon his students, that action and reaction go hand in hand, and if this mysterious power or influence is used for improper or evil purposes, it will sooner or later react with greater force upon the one using it, for—

"Whoso diggeth a pit shall fall therein, and he that rolleth a stone, it shall return upon him." —(Prov. 26:27.)

It is sincerely hoped by the author, both for the sake of the science and the public good, that all who learn and realize the wonderful advantage a Hypnotist has, will never take advantage or abuse the power he has had placed in his hands by a knowledge of the science of Hypnotism and Mesmerism.

Some of the results which have been described and some of the statements which have been made in this work may seem so startling that the author can quite easily understand their being received by some with a certain degree of suspicion. Indeed, in all psychic phenomena the more enlightened and scientific minds will naturally demand at least to see demonstrations of these phenomena before they yield their absolute credence. However, it is not my intention or duty to convince any one, but only to record facts which I know from personal experience and observation to be true.

Prof. L. W. DeLaurence.

CHAPTER XXXIII.

TREATMENT BY HYPNOTISM AND SUGGESTION.

1. Rheumatism.—2. Articular Rheumatism.—3. Menorrhagia.—4. Paralysis Arm and Leg.—5. Habitual Drunkard.—6. Insomnia.—7. Chronic Rheumatism.—8. Aggravated Hysteria.—9. Cigarette Habit.—10. Moral Depravity.—11. Child Birth.—12. Stammering Cured by Hypnotism.

In this chapter are given extracts of a few of the large number of cases successfully treated by Suggestive Therapeutics or Hypnotic Suggestion, by the author.

CASE No. 1—Rheumatism, pains in the shoulder joints, arms and lower limbs for almost three years.

James C. C., aged 47, an employe of iron mills, a man of good physique and had always enjoyed good health excepting one or two attacks of sciatica about two years before chronic rheumatism set in.

At the time he came for treatment by Hypnotic Suggestion, the pains were pronounced in both shoulders, especially the left one, at the point where the collar bone articulates with the scapula. There was also a decided lameness just above the anterior superior spine of the ilium on the right side, and which was noticed most when stooping over or bending forward.

The patient also suffered intense pains in both knees and ankle joints. After explaining the possibilities of treatment by Suggestion I proceeded to induce sleep by the Mesmeric passes and suggestion.

The patient soon fell into a deep, quiet sleep, and while in this condition was given reasonable but decided suggestions that he would feel an agreeable and warm influence passing all over his body, from my hands, which held both of his; that this influence would drive out all ache and pain from his diseased joints, and that when awakened he would have no pain whatever in any part of his body.

After being awakened in the regular manner the pains in his knees and ankles were gone, as were also those in the back and shoulders. For months previous to the treatment by Suggestion the patient had been unable to walk without a cane, but could do so now with ease.

Four days after he was again Hypnotized and given suggestions as before. The third treatment was given a few days later, and the last one in about a week, from which he awoke entirely cured, and has remained so since.

CASE No. 2—Articular rheumatism for seven months. Cured by Hypnotism and Suggestion inside of ten days.

Miss Carrie S., aged 20. This young lady was brought to the hotel in a carriage while I was giving some demonstrations in a well known city in Canada, her parents having learned that relief possibly might be obtained for their daughter by Suggestive treatment.

It was necessary for the patient to be supported by her parents from the carriage to the hotel parlor, she being weak and pale and quite unable to stand or walk alone, having had several severe attacks of hysteria.

For some time before she had suffered greatly from sub-acute rheumatism, which had become gradually and steadily worse.

Upon examination it was found that both wrists and finger joints were badly swollen and acutely painful upon pressure. The lower limbs were also swollen and very sensitive, with pain and inflammation at the ankles. The spine was decidedly affected, there also being present leucorrhoea and amenorrhoea, the patient being troubled with nervousness and inability to sleep at night.

The first induction of Hypnosis was entirely successful and the patient went into a deep sleep. Then the proper suggestions for relief and improvement were given. After the second treatment, which she received upon the following day, the patient rested well at night, and had a decided improvement in her appetite.

The swelling at the joints had almost entirely disappeared, there being only a slight soreness present on pressure.

Two days later she was again Hypnotized and suggestions given that she would awake free from pain and feel greatly strengthened in mind and body, and that she would not feel any more pain.

She was Hypnotized twice afterwards and became completely well and cured of all undesirable symptoms, and was able to walk or ride her wheel without fatigue or pain, and altogether seemed like a changed young lady both in mind and body.

CASE No. 3—Menorrhagia every twelve or fifteen days' time extended to four weeks and eventually cured.

Mrs. W., aged 30, mother of two children, the

youngest being four years old. Hysterical and of poor constitution. Previous to her first pregnancy the period had been regular every four weeks, but for the last three years it had returned about every twelve or fifteen days, and sometimes, if worried or overworked, at shorter intervals.

The flow being very copious and accompanied by pain in the spine and at the base of the brain. During the first treatment she readily entered into a deep degree of sleep, then decided suggestions were given that she would gradually improve in health and mind, and that the next period would not come on until four weeks, and that the flow would only be of three days' duration, and positively would be unaccompanied by any pain or anxiety.

The treatment was given immediately after her last period. Fifteen days later she felt premonitory symptoms of its return. She was again Hypnotized and by suggestion these symptoms and pains were made to pass off, and by suggestion, repeated every four days, the period was retarded until the four weeks were up. The flow lasted three days, was unattended by any pain and less copious than usual.

Her next treatment was given three days after the period had ceased and suggestions given that the next period would not come on until four weeks from the last, and henceforth every four weeks.

It did not appear again until four weeks from the last, and as the previous period, was free from pain and lasted about three days.

The treatment was continued every nine days for three months, at the end of which time the function was thoroughly regulated, and occurred every twenty-seven or eight days, unattended by pain or other abnormal condition.

During the treatment other nervous disorders and minor symptoms with which the patient had been troubled disappeared.

CASE No. 4—Paralysis of the right arm and leg.

J. H., aged 40, was a well-built man, with an originally strong constitution, being a blacksmith by trade.

The first symptoms appeared about two years ago. Fourteen months later he suddenly lost all power of his right arm and leg.

At the time he consulted me he was suffering from severe pains in the neck and right shoulder, which had been present about five weeks. This pain prevented him securing more than two or three hours sleep at night. The trouble was of syphilitic origin, but anti-syphilitic treatment had produced no desirable effect for some time.

The patient was neither able to raise his arm or foot, or extend his fingers, seeming to have no control over the afflicted members.

He was Mesmerized by the use of passes and suggestion, a deep stage of Hypnosis being induced. Then suggestions were given for the relief of the pain, and the rigidity of the paralyzed limbs were relaxed by favorable suggestions, and active movements of the arm and leg.

That the patient would feel a sense of warmth passing down through his paralyzed limbs, that when he awoke the pain would be greatly lessened, and that upon retiring he would immediately go into a sound sleep and have a good night's rest.

Upon awakening the pain in his neck and shoulder was found to be greatly relieved, and that night he, for the first time in months, slept soundly.

The patient was Hypnotized twice a week for two months. Two weeks after the treatment was begun all pain had disappeared and he was able to sleep from seven to nine hours every night.

During Hypnosis artificial movements of the arm and leg were employed and in time the patient could move them himself when suggestions were given him to do so, and the power of life and vital forces gradually returned to the limbs, so that at the end of four weeks the man could open and close his hand, and raise his arm on a level with the shoulder, retaining it in this horizontal position for a short time.

The treatments were continued and after eight weeks he could move his arm and hand at will, and could walk with ease, his right limb being strong enough to support his body.

CASE No. 5—Habitual drunkard.

H. B., tailor by occupation, a man 30 years of age, and an expert workman, but for seven years drank whiskey to excess, which had brought on several attacks of delirium tremens, so that his mind or mental forces had greatly deteriorated.

The desire for strong drink had so overcome his will power that he had absolutely no resistance left.

After being Hypnotized he was given suggestions that he would have a decided abhorrence for whiskey, and that even the smell of it would disgust and sicken him; that when he awoke he would have his power of mind and will greatly increased and strengthened and would once more know and realize that he was possessed of manhood enough to keep from disgracing himself and family.

He was further induced to give a solemn pledge that he would drink no more whiskey or stimulants. He was given suggestions of this nature daily for a week, then twice a week for two weeks, then once a week for a month. And after that no suggestions were necessary.

After the first Hypnosis he did not take a drink of whiskey or alcoholic liquor of any kind, although it was offered him several different times.

Four weeks after the treatment began he was given employment by one of his former employers who had discharged him for drinking. This act greatly encouraged and strengthened his intention to again be a man, and there is scarcely any question but what he will always be able to lead a temperate life.

CASE No. 6—Insomnia.

M. D., a dentist, aged about 40 years, whose general health had become badly affected because of an inability to sleep. His sleeplessness dated from a severe accident, he being thrown from a buggy during a runaway, having his head badly injured. He was a man of exceptional intelligence, and the want of sleep had brought on decided nervous depression and dyspepsia.

At whatever time he retired he was unable to go to sleep and would roll and toss about until his efforts to sleep almost drove him frantic, and would scarcely ever secure over an hour's troubled rest during the night, rising in the morning weak and nervous.

He was quite easily put to sleep, and highly susceptible to suggestion, any part of his body becoming cataleptic by suggestion.

After getting him perfectly under control I gave suggestions that as soon as he went to bed that night he would close his eyes and feel a sleepy, drowsy sensation creeping all over his body, that every nerve and muscle would be resting perfectly quiet, and that he would go sound asleep and not wake up until morning.

These suggestions were repeated several times. The next day he reported having had the first good night's sleep since the accident.

The treatment was continued every second day for two weeks, which completed the course. Since that time he has continued to sleep well at night. His mind and health have also improved to a corresponding degree.

This case is one of special interest, as this

morbid habit of long standing was successfully cured in about two weeks by Suggestion.

CASE No. 7—Chronic rheumatism.

Lucy H., aged 27, was sent to me to be cured. She was suffering from rheumatism in both shoulders and arms. It had troubled her for over a year, causing great pain when she moved her arms, so that she could not comb her hair or dress herself. The lameness had come on gradually and had resisted all previous attempts to cure it.

She readily entered a deep stage of Hypnosis, and while in that state I gave suggestions that all pain and lameness was leaving her body, and that when she awoke she would be free from pain and again have use of her arms and hands.

Her arms were also rubbed and passes made downward while the suggestions were being given. Upon awakening she seemed to have better use of her arms but had some slight pain left in the shoulder.

Three days later she was again put to sleep, this time during Hypnosis I gave her a broom and made her sweep the floor, suggesting that she had no pain whatever in her arms. She handled the broom with ease, then after giving suggestion that she would be entirely free from pain I aroused her, no pain being present. She remained under treatment for two weeks, and at the end of that time returned to her work as a domestic, absolutely free of pain.

CASE No. 8—Aggravated hysteria of over five years standing cured by Hypnotism and Suggestion in six weeks.

Mrs. W., aged 34, mother of two children. A woman of good constitution and lively but nervous temperament. She had never noticed any symptoms of hysteria until about five years ago.

After the first few attacks they increased in frequency and were more severe. They occurred about every three weeks and were accompanied by a depressed condition of mind, and by a sense of constriction at the throat. These premonitory symptoms were followed by fretful crying spells which usually lasted about a day.

Following this came general muscular tremors which increased to strong convulsive movements, alternating with decided rigidity of the whole body.

The attack lasted from fifteen to forty minutes, and after passing off would leave the patient weak and exhausted. Sometimes she would have five or six spells, as they termed them, in twenty-four hours.

At the first induction of Hypnotism she fell into a light nervous sleep. After giving suggestions to quiet her mind, she entered into a profound sleep. Then she was given suggestions that there would not be a return of the spells, that she would enjoy a more cheerful condition of mind and would not think or worry about their return, that every day her nervous system would grow stronger and that she would know and realize that they would not return again.

At the end of six weeks she was completely cured and has remained free from hysteria ever since.

CASE No. 9—Cigarette habit cured.

Charlie M., a young man of 20, was sent to me to be cured of the cigarette habit. He was the son of a prominent railroad official, and had smoked cigarettes continuously for about three years. His father had tried to break him of the habit, and the young man had made frequent attempts himself, but had relapsed each time, the intense desire to smoke being so great that he could not resist it. When he came for treatment he was in a highly nervous condition, palpitation of the heart being present, as was also mental irritability, dyspepsia and catarrh, all due to the large number of cigarettes he had been in the habit of smoking.

I first proceeded to fasten his hands together in the regular way, then quickly threw him into a deep stage of Hypnosis, and by suggestion placed his mind in a quiet receptive condition, telling him to listen very carefully to every word I said to him. I then stated to him that when he woke up he would have entirely ceased to care for cigarettes, that he would become disgusted at the sight of one, and that the odor from them would be so obnoxious and offensive to him that he would rather take a snake in his hand than touch another cigarette.

I then induced somnambulism, and while in this state offered him a cigarette. He absolutely refused to take one, and when I slipped a box of them in his coat pocket he instantly threw them on the floor, saying he would rather have a snake in his pocket than those horrible things.

I then stated to him that as long as he lived he would never have anything but disgust and contempt for cigarettes. These suggestions were repeated every afternoon for two weeks. Also other suggestions were given in regard to the improvement of his general health. From the first treatment the young man could not be induced to touch or smoke another cigarette, so complete was his dislike for them.

His health improved very rapidly and today he is entirely free from any symptoms of cigarette smoking or desire for them.

CASE No. 10—Moral depravity of long standing cured by Hypnotism and Suggestion.

S. L., a young man of 22, sent to me to be Hypnotized and treated by Suggestion, by a well known physician, a friend of mine, who had considerable knowledge as to the possibilities of Hypnotism, and knew that morbid habits of this nature require psychical treatment, as all ordinary treatment, either medical or surgical, fail to cure these vices.

Psychology teaches us that these perverted sexual instincts are the result of an hereditary or acquired morbid condition of the mind, and constitute, strictly speaking, a psychical disease. And require for their cure psychic treatment (Hypnotic Suggestion), which entirely changes the diseased mental condition or depraved desire to practice masturbation, the mind being strengthened and reinforced by Suggestion during Hypnosis.

If Hypnotism and Suggestion has done nothing more for mankind than to bring these deplorable cases, which contaminate many young men and women of today, within the scope of curative treatment, it most certainly has conferred a great blessing and lasting benefit upon misguided humanity, as they are far more prevalent than is generally supposed outside of the medical profession and insane asylum.

This young man who had practiced this demoralizing and private vice since early manhood, and which had brought him to a deplorable mental and physical condition, verging on insanity, was without special effort placed under the influence of Hypnotism. Suggestions (decided) were then given to change his condition of mind and bring him face to face with a full realization of his acts, and what they would ultimately bring him to. And to remove this inhuman desire, greatly increasing will power and self-control. He came every other day for treatment and at the expiration of two weeks all influence and desire of the habit had disappeared.

For success in these cases it is essential for the physician or operator to secure the patient's confidence, letting him understand that you are and will take a personal interest in his welfare and good.

And that you wish him to unite and enter into

a common effort with you for the betterment of his condition and health.

These patients should be closely watched, for they are notoriously given to deception. But one can secure their confidence by careful, judicious management, and then they are saved the danger of permitting "the wish to be father to the thought, or desire."

They fully realize their utter helplessness and gladly welcome any encouraging word or helping hand, if properly presented.

CASE No. 11—Child birth.

Mrs. B., aged 24. In this case I was called to use Hypnotism and Suggestion at the wish of the patient, who had been in labor for twenty-eight hours.

The labor pains had ceased and she was suffering a continuous pain, being almost completely exhausted when I arrived.

The head was upon the perineum, and still in the pelvis, having remained there for over two hours without any change or advance. I secured the patient's attention and quickly induced Hypnosis; gave suggestions to remove the pain and all sense of fatigue.

Then I told her the labor was prolonged and due to certain causes, that she would know and realize that the child was being born and would be conscious of everything that was done, but would not suffer or feel any pain, and that she would remain quiet and calm as possible, and not struggle or worry.

I then told her to close her eyes and bear down hard when told to do so. The physician then proceeded and with the use of forceps brought the head through the pelvis. Then she was given suggestion to bear down hard, but that no pain whatever would be felt.

The child was delivered painlessly, as was the placenta. After being brought out from the influence of Suggestion the mother stated that she had felt no pain and was well pleased that she had been saved a great amount of suffering.

CASE No. 12—Stammering cured by Hypnotic Suggestion.

L. S., aged 22. This young man had been all through his life unable to speak a word without stammering or hesitating. He had been sent by his parents to different institutions to be cured, but returned each time very little improved, and would shortly relapse into his old way and stammer about every word he attempted to speak.

At the second induction of Hypnosis a deep stage was obtained. Then he was given suggestions that his affliction was not due to any abnormal condition of the vocal organs but was the result of an actual condition of his mind, and that when this impression was removed he could and would speak without stammering.

Somnambulism was then induced and decided and convincing suggestions were given that he would not stammer or hesitate when he spoke. That he would know and realize in his own mind that he had the ability and power to speak his words without hesitating, that he now would have confidence in himself, and that when he approached a person he would talk to him without becoming confused or losing self-control; and that when he attempted to converse over the 'phone he would do so without confusion.

He was engaged in ordinary conversation after these suggestions had been given him and was able to speak and pronounce certain words which he had always hesitated over, such words, for instance, as those beginning with s and f.

Then while in this condition he was sent to a telephone and, calling up a lady friend, he talked to her by wire, a thing he had never been able to do before.

Decided Post-Hypnotic Suggestions were then given in regard to the morrow and at all future time he would and could speak without stammering, and that he would find a wonderful improvement in his speech. That all words beginning with s and f would be found quite easy for him to pronounce.

Treatment was given daily in this case for three weeks; with an encouraging improvement from the first induction of Hypnosis. At the end of this time the young man was able to speak fluently and greatly surprised his parents and acquaintances by his being cured of stammering.

THE END.